T0152308

POWER **RECRUITING**

POWER
RECRUITING

EFFECTIVELY HIRE
THE BEST TALENT
IN YOUR INDUSTRY

DIANA Y. JI

NEW YORK

LONDON • NASHVILLE • MELBOURNE • VANCOUVER

POWER **RECRUITING**
EFFECTIVELY HIRE THE BEST TALENT
IN YOUR INDUSTRY

© 2021 **DIANA Y. JI**

All rights reserved. No portion of this book may be reproduced, stored in a retrieval system, or transmitted in any form or by any means—electronic, mechanical, photocopy, recording, scanning, or other—except for brief quotations in critical reviews or articles, without the prior written permission of the publisher.

Published in New York, New York, by Morgan James Publishing in partnership with Difference Press. Morgan James is a trademark of Morgan James, LLC.
www.MorganJamesPublishing.com

ISBN 978-1-63195-230-2 paperback
ISBN 978-1-63195-231-9 eBook
ISBN 978-1-63195-232-6 audio
Library of Congress Control Number: 2020909280

Cover Design Concept:
Nakita Duncan

Editor:
Emily Tuttle

Book Coaching:
The Author Incubator

Morgan James is a proud partner of Habitat for Humanity Peninsula and Greater Williamsburg. Partners in building since 2006.

Get involved today! Visit
www.MorganJamesBuilds.com

To Charlotte and Hamilton,
who inspire me every day.

TABLE OF CONTENTS

CHAPTER 1
SIMON'S FRUSTRATION

Simon is an energetic vice president of clinical development at Genetec Bio Science (GBS), a promising biotech company based out of Boston. He joined the company in late 2018 to lead a robust clinical development organization. GBS was established in 2008 with a vision to become a key player in the rare diseases area in order to serve patients' unmet needs. Simon was recruited to this newly created role from New Jersey after a successful stint at another biotech company, where he served for eight years as the director of clinical development. Simon was referred by a colleague he used to work with who had become the head of the procurement at GBS. The interview process went quite smoothly, and the GBS team was impressed by Simon's leadership skills and experience in global clinical development across all phases of drug development.

Generally speaking, Simon's new role at GBS checked all the boxes of what his ideal career would be: it was at a rapidly growing company with a great vision set forth by its founders, he was working with a highly talented team with a nimble organizational structure, and he had the autonomy to make decisions to shape his team. He was also part of the senior leadership team and able to influence the direction of the company.

After settling in for a few months at GBS, things were going in the direction Simon envisioned. The founder and president had a superior business background and set forth an exemplary vision for the company. Though quite demanding, Simon's boss was also a good listener and supportive of Simon's work. Additionally, the people at GBS were amazing. Simon interacted with a lot of senior staff members in research and development, and they all seemed to be extremely bright. Ninety percent of the scientists on his team had PhDs, and some of them had graduated from top schools. Simon was really inspired by working with them.

Though the company did not have any FDA-approved drugs yet, the results of early clinical development seemed quite positive. Employee morale was quite high, as was the energy at the workplace. People talked positively about the culture of the company, their managers, and their peers. Rare disease was one of the areas Simon wanted to focus on in his career, as he really hoped that by doing so, he would make a bigger impact in patients' lives. The company's direction, science, and vision all made Simon's daily work life fun to experience.

On the other hand, Simon faced a lot of challenges. Since the company was a pretty flat organization, he had quite a large team reporting directly to him. So, he worked with his HR business partner to redesign the team structure. A few years ago, the clinical development team was primarily using contractors and vendors to provide services. Over the past year or two, however, he converted most of the contractors to permanent employees. Simon had five direct reports, all at director to senior director levels, most of whom were promoted from within. These directors did not have extensive managerial experience when they started with GBS, but they gained that from working their way up.

Facing the company's rapid growth, over the next two years, Simon expected more of these employees to continue to step up and develop new skill sets quickly. But Simon felt that his managers lacked strong managerial experience. The scope of the responsibilities under certain directors was still quite narrow, compared to what Simon was used to seeing from his previous company.

Beginning in 2019, Simon was approved for five full-time headcounts at the director level, but only three were hired. Out of those three, Simon got a resignation from one of them, who received a fantastic VP offer at a startup company in California. He was one of Simon's key senior directors, and it was really hard to see him leave when he was such a crucial employee.

The three new senior-level positions on Simon's team, in addition to the other continuing challenges from the business end, put a strain on the team's resources. In the senior leadership meetings that Simon attended, the company confirmed it had an ambitious growth plan. It would increase its clinical development by another 80 percent in 2019 and expected to have its first drug approved by late 2020 or 2021. In other words, Simon's team would continue to expand at least another 40 to 50 percent in the next two years, adding three or more director-level positions in 2020. Simon needed to hire at least two senior directors of clinical development and one director of clinical operations, in addition to other mid-level managers on his team.

"Where can I find these people?" Simon asked himself during his short coffee break between his morning meetings. "And where can I find them quickly, by March of this year?" He paused and frowned.

No doubt, Simon was concerned about recruiting. This was not his area of expertise, yet his organizational goals would be very much affected by whether he could staff the right people and onboard them quickly.

Simon was a bit frustrated about the previous year's recruiting results as well. Not only was this not his area of expertise, but he did not feel he had much time for recruiting. Simon's calendar was typically booked up with meetings and business travel up to two weeks in advance. For example, this morning alone he attended four meetings, including a meeting with the project development team and a senior leadership meeting with the CEO. Simon knew that HR called him at different times, and he still needed to find a time to reply back to them.

Simon had a dedicated talent acquisition specialist and HR business partner supporting the clinical development department. They were both pleasant to work with and had rich experience with HR and recruiting in the biopharma industry. He trusted them, and he expected them to take care of finding the talent. If Simon were asked what areas of the hiring process he would change, he would probably say that he wished to review higher-quality résumés and interview candidates he really liked, not spend time with candidates that he wasn't really excited about.

With twenty-five years of experience in biopharma and twenty years of leadership experience, Simon also knew that yes, he was judgmental. He expected to only interview the best candidates within his busy schedule, and he expected the people he brought on to complement what he had already assembled on his team. He wanted these candidates to have a strong passion for what the company did (rare diseases) and be energized and motivated by working in a smaller company. He wanted to see candidates who not only focused on short-term gains but also aimed for long-term growth. Simon wanted to see talents who were the top stars at their current companies, the most driven, talented, and energized talents that almost every hiring manager dreams of. Above all these, he expected candidates to come in sooner rather than later for the interviews. He expected candidates he really liked—like the one he met with last month—to accept the GBS offer in the end. In Simon's ideal world, these expectations would all be met.

In reality, Simon received ten résumés from HR since his five positions opened up within a month. This wasn't bad; however, after reading the résumés carefully, Simon did not want to interview some of them, and some candidates he did want to interview backed out and got different offers from other biotech companies. After two months, Simon ended up interviewing three people, and bringing two on-site. One was really good, and one was disappointing after the face-to-face meeting.

The candidate Simon really liked was not approved of by everyone. Some of the people on the interview panel expressed concerns, but Simon went ahead and extended an offer anyway. After two rounds of offer negotiation with HR (adding an additional three weeks in the process), the candidate turned down the final offer and decided to work for another company.

Simon's reality was three months of searching and no hires. Simon was quite disappointed. He realized that he needed to start the recruiting process all over again with HR. His extensive business travels throughout September and October, and the holiday seasons in November and December, didn't make it easy. Without a doubt, Simon wished for a good recruitment year. This was the year Simon would be focusing on building his team and establishing his leadership.

Simon thought about the need to recruit candidates for a few seconds while drinking his coffee, rang HR, and left a voicemail. Everyone was busy in the company—there was never idle time—but he needed to keep moving forward with recruiting.

With that, Simon started a new email to his HR talent acquisition specialist, Jennifer, and copied his HR business partner, Kevin.

Subject: Recruiting for 2020
Jennifer and Kevin,
Happy 2020!
I would like to schedule a meeting together to kick off our recruiting in 2020. Let's brainstorm how we can meet our staffing needs. As last updated in December 2019, we still have two remaining positions and one recent resignation. When we

have our headcount approved next week, my reserved estimate is about fifteen for my department this year by then.

 How soon we can meet up to discuss?

 Regards,

 Simon

Five minutes later, Simon got an email from Jennifer and Kevin:

 Simon,

 Happy New Year!

 Love to meet, and we definitely have new ideas to propose. Let's meet this afternoon, if you are available, 4—5 p.m.

 Jennifer and Kevin

With the kick-off meeting between business, recruiting, and HR set, 2020 recruiting at GBS has turned to a new chapter. Simon is looking forward to the meeting and envisions shaking hands with his new team members in the coming months. His team needs people, and together, they have big goals to accomplish this year.

CHAPTER 2
MY JOURNEY AS A RECRUITER TO BONGENE SEARCH

When I was in my early twenties, one of the hardest decisions I faced was choosing a profession. I always wanted to be a journalist, as I loved to write and liked to connect with people. However, my education did not really provide me with the tools and background required to become a journalist. So, I got into HR, and then recruiting later, without a plan; in retrospect, all the dots connected and led to the path that I am taking today.

Upon graduating from Zhongshan University in Guangdong, China, as an English major, I submitted my résumé through campus recruiting to the Walmart Asia headquarters, Shenzhen office, in the spring of 2000.

After a few rounds of interviews, I received an offer as a management trainee in their HR department, a field that I almost blindly chose. At that time, I was preparing for my GRE exam to apply for graduate school in the United States. I did not think I would work in China for a long time but, rather, just wanted to find a job to support myself while I worked on the graduate school application. I also thought that working would help me figure out what I was good at and would ultimately help me decide what kind of jobs I should stick to. However, those three years working in China turned out to be one of the most worthwhile experiences in my career and my life.

The Walmart Asia headquarters started its management trainee program around 1999, three years after the corporation established its business entity in China, to meet the increasing need for well-trained management talent. I selected HR as my first choice department because I thought I would really enjoy working with people, even though I didn't know exactly what human resources meant at the time. Luckily enough, the HR department also selected me, and I became one of their four management trainees.

The HR management trainee program at Walmart was a fantastic experience. We spent six months in corporate and at stores learning about the business, helping with HR programs, talking to associates, and greeting Walmart customers. Even today, I remember Walmart cheers and the clapping hands ritual employees did to boost the energy when they got together and planned to start a meeting. Walmart has a strong culture, and it was a great example of how people and business can link together and form a legendary company.

After six months of the business rotational program with Walmart, I started my first HR specialist role in employee relations and then was later asked to help with recruiting. I was my manager's right-hand person, and I was a fast learner. I quickly learned to conduct interviews and always recommended the right people for the job. In my first year, our team hired a few hundred employees. The company quickly expanded in China and recruiting talent was the number-one HR priority.

After two years working in corporate HR, I wanted to try something different. At the time, the field of executive searching and recruiting was just starting out in China, and there were not many experienced professionals in the field yet. Naturally curious, I decided to give it a try, so I joined a new, internet-based recruiting company as part of its newly created executive-retained search team.

I remember my boss, David, interviewed me in his office after the end of my workday. I was offered the job on the spot and started working three weeks later. My role at the time was not only to recruit for senior-level talent but also to find clients who needed top talent. I had no book or instructions on how to do this kind of work, so

I relied on my own research, starting with one cold-call client and developing our list from there. I just focused on one client at a time while making sure that I gave them the best service, and they kept hiring me and referring me to other people in the industry.

In no time, I grew my recruiting business steadily and quickly.

The business was 100 percent retained, and my new clients asked, "How can I trust you when we have not worked with you and we are asked to pay the retainer up front?"

Instead of answering them directly, I asked them what they really wanted and then explained how I thought I could help. I remember there was a client who needed an Asia-Pacific finance director and the role had been open for three months. He wanted someone with very strong leadership experience across Asia-Pacific markets in the consumer packaged goods (CPG) field. I related my Walmart recruiting experience to this and convinced the vice president at the time to hire us. I worked day and night for that search and contacted more than one hundred finance directors in Shenzhen and nearby cities.

At that time, there was no LinkedIn or any other authoritative database, so I researched all the major CPG companies and mapped out their finance directors' information. Oftentimes their profiles were not public due to the nature of their roles. Throughout the entire sourcing and recruiting process, I visualized this director of finance working in his office and the ideal talent that I should pursue. To this day, this visualization process is the start of all my searches. It gives me unwavering confidence that the top talent can be identified and hired.

Back to that particular search—through my hard work, a few strong candidates were presented within the first week and one of those eventually got hired. Once I did well with this client, I received a lot of referrals, and my business continued to grow from there. I had an amazing first year in the executive search industry. I was the top recruiter on the national team against forty-plus veteran recruiters. Focus, dedication, and confidence in my ability to serve my clients helped me succeed in my first year.

After working in the executive search industry for about a year, I came to know about Korn Ferry, the best and largest executive search company in the world, through an article I read about its newly hired country manager in China. Since I was doing well in the search industry, I was motivated about pursuing a career in the executive search industry, with an idea that one day I wanted to work with a company like Korn Ferry.

Fast-forward two years, and I flew to the United States to spend two years at Rutgers University, pursuing a Master's degree in its Human Resource Management Program. The program was about designing the right HR strategies and practices for businesses. What I most enjoyed about the program was learning through many case studies about different companies' HR strategies and then designing our own. Designing the HR scorecard to align with the business scorecard was one of the highlights of the program.

After I graduated, I had an opportunity to work in Korn Ferry's Beijing office but decided to stay in the United States to grow my family, as I had just gotten married. Over the next few years, I worked as an HR consultant in the high-tech and pharmaceutical industries. Still, in the back of my mind, I knew one day I would go back to executive search and start my own search firm.

In 2008, I took a recruiting job with a well-known agency to support my growing family in Philadelphia. I worked in the high-tech and life science sectors, which were fast growing, and the needs for senior-level talent were very strong. I worked so hard for the job, as if it were the only opportunity I had. I quickly became the go-to recruiter to support difficult roles that came to the national team. I was pregnant with my second child at the time, and I remember asking my manager if I could work from home for some time when it was needed. The answer was that all employees were expected to work in the office.

Two years later, when I relocated to New York with my family, the same manager said I could work 100 percent remotely because she did not want to lose me on the team. To this day, I appreciate the flexible working schedule she extended to me. I was able to spend more time with my young toddlers by saving commute time. The non-office environment gave me a much-needed break from my always busy schedule to think more about what I wanted to do next professionally. The week before I started my own search firm three years later, she asked me if I wanted to work for her client as a senior recruiter.

I said, "Sorry, maybe next time."

After working as a successful recruiter in a competitive agency environment, I was very clear that I wanted to build my own recruiting firm soon. However, I didn't feel the time was right yet. I wanted to specialize in one particular industry and really know the ins and outs of that industry before starting. Then one day, I received a phone call from a company that was hiring a recruiter for Regeneron Pharmaceuticals, the Google of biotech. I knew this was the job for me to take.

It surely was. I had a great time working there. *Science* magazine has named Regeneron the number-one biopharma employer six years in a row because of its unparalleled leadership team, rigorous science, and strong sense of social responsibility. The company had just started its growth spurt when I was hired.

As a talent acquisition specialist, I partnered with the senior-level managers and executives, learned about their business, and solved their hiring needs through my recruiting expertise. I learned so much from working with these talented people and enjoyed the partnership and achieving the talent acquisition goals together. During my two years there, I supported various corporate, commercial, and clinical functions.

Take a regulatory affairs recruiting project for example. The hiring manager, who was the head of the department, liked to use many agencies at the same time in hopes that he would get the best talent quickly. Because he kept getting candidates from agencies, he continued to work with them directly without the internal recruiting team's involvement, which was not normal HR procedure.

This actually created a lot of problems, including miscommunication about the roles and candidates among the external recruiting partner, internal recruiter, and the hiring manager and massive inconsistencies in the hiring process.

On the other hand, I totally understood why the hiring manager liked to send jobs to those specialized agencies as soon as they were open, especially to the ones that had provided great talent to him in the past. He trusted that they could fill these jobs quickly and effectively and that these specialized agencies could find "hidden talent" who were not normally applying for any jobs or did not even have public LinkedIn profiles. In short, he trusted these agencies could give him the results that he expected in a timely fashion. Good agencies are able to fulfill those needs, of course. This is what they do!

Understanding his expectations and recruiting requirements, as well as knowing how competitive the regulatory talent market was, I asked the hiring manager to give me the first two weeks to learn each agency's strengths and capabilities, select the best ones to work with, and streamline the process for everyone involved. He agreed and was very generous in sharing the business knowledge that I very much needed to recruit effectively in the regulatory field. In making this shift, I asked him to trust me in leading the recruiting process because in the end, I wanted to save him time recruiting while still getting the best people to work on his team.

Our goals were essentially the same—hiring the best and hiring effectively. Subsequently, I found myself speaking with all the agencies he worked with, interviewing them, and selecting and recommending the top two to him. In the end, we selected one to work with. We then developed a close partnership to work together under a streamlined recruiting process, which was simpler and more focused. I made sure that the agency was treated as an extension of my recruiting team. Trust and working closely are the keys to any successful partnership and critical to getting the job done effectively. Recruiting is a partnership and a team effort. All parties' goals become one goal, and then everything becomes easier.

As a new recruiter on the talent acquisition team in a corporate setting, I wanted to fill these positions without using external agencies. However, I quickly realized that using specialized agencies would be the most time-efficient way to recruit in niche areas. Not only do they have massive candidate reach and database, but they also have had years to build relationships with these candidates and recruit nationally for other leading companies in the same industry. They have tremendous insights about talent (the supply side) in a particular field as well as all the competitors (the demand side). There has been an increasing imbalance of the supply and demand of talent, especially in high-tech and biotech industries. It is a global challenge. I have nothing but respect for those highly successful and ethical executive search firms that make recruiting a truly fascinating craft.

While I exceled as a talent acquisition partner in-house serving this fast-growing biotech company in New York, I realized that my role had inevitably become corporate-driven and sometimes heavily focused on the administrative aspects of recruiting rather than strategizing on how to best fill positions.

I saw myself as being more of an entrepreneur and maybe more of a "free spirit." After acquiring all the experience I had in the biotech industry and learning from others, including good and not so good agencies, I knew it was a time to run my own search firm. I could do a better job than those firms out there! I knew the recruiting part was easy, but putting together business was more of an uncertainty and unknown to me. But I didn't care too much. I just wanted to continue to serve my clients better, even though I didn't know where my clients were. I knew if I was good at recruiting, I could recruit my own clients for sure!

The idea of starting my own firm really resonated with me and motivated me. I started immediately by quitting my job the next day, registering a domain name, and signing up for an email address that I could use. Of course, there were many more small and major projects necessary to start a business, but I couldn't wait to get started.

In 2014, shortly after we moved from New York to New Jersey, I officially started Bongene Search. *Bon* means "good" in French, and *gene* is a reference to the DNA molecule, indicating we are associated with the biotech industry and also implying our "people" focus. Recruiting is fascinating to me because it is all about people and people are the most dynamic factor. After all my years spent in HR and recruiting within these fast-changing environments, I felt I was ready to develop a proprietary system to serve more biotech companies, with better business results. I was also excited about developing a company that is nimble and focused on change and learning so that it stays competitive in this field.

Just as with any other startup company, the first few steps were the most difficult and yet the most critical. In the early days, we were unknown in the industry, and we had to compete with bigger agencies for business. I remember there was a recruiting engagement by one of the top biopharma companies in the world. We signed up for their agencies portal and the positions were released to all the agencies on that portal. They selected ten agencies to work on four director-level market access roles. I didn't care about our competitors. What I focused on at the start of the business was what we did, how we could be the best at what we did, what tools we could use, and what strategies and tactics we could implement.

We focused on recruiting for these positions with laser-like attention. We implemented well-thought-out and competitive recruiting strategies so that I could cover the majority of the talent in the market, including passive and hidden ones. It does not sound like a big deal, but when you put all these strategies together, we were winning in the game, and we were the most efficient. After two weeks of relentless recruiting, we presented eleven director-level candidates to our clients. In the end, we received four offers and three were accepted immediately. One offer was rejected, but we had another backup candidate, so another offer was extended and then taken!

Our stellar performance wowed our clients. One of the recruiting directors paid us the retainer using her own credit card because she wanted us to continuously work with them and start our process ASAP. There have been numerous times when we fulfilled our clients' hiring needs quickly and effectively. After five years, my first client still works with us. In fact, all of our clients are still with us today because of the trust we have developed over the years. My nature doesn't allow me to let my clients down. I always strive to meet and exceed their expectations by working hard and smart.

The year 2020 marks my twentieth year in recruiting. I thought writing a book would be a good recap for me personally and professionally to reflect on my journey as a recruiter. Most importantly, I believe I could share with you, my dear reader, a few tips and some wisdom that I have learned so far in this field.

CHAPTER 3
THE POWER ROAD MAP

The goal of this book is to help you, either the hiring manager or recruiter, build a successful hiring process and to instruct you on how to implement the best hiring practices. These concepts and practices are ones that I have employed during my time working within hiring teams in the biopharmaceutical industry and with leading biopharmaceutical firms as an outside recruiter in their hiring process. By adhering to these practices and policies, you will have a more dynamic and fluid hiring process. Crucially, this will be a hiring process that brings in top-quality talent who fit the role in an efficient manner.

Recruiting is a team effort and it is a result-driven process that typically lasts weeks or months. At the end, we complete it by putting the right people in the right positions so they create value for the company. In my mind, I always view recruiting as a journey. So, we start off by setting a road map.

In this chapter, I will provide an overview of our Power Road Map. This is a system that we have developed to hire the best talent in the biopharma industry. Certain strategies may be applicable to other industries as well. You will learn different aspects of these strategies at a high-level and how these strategies work separately to help people and organizations achieve their recruiting goals.

Recruiting is a highly collaborative process, meant to put the best talent in its most suitable position. In the sector we serve, most of the talent has been in the industry for over ten years. Not only are they experienced, but their level in the corporation's chain of command is also quite high, at least senior manager or above. Many of these candidates have received rigorous academic training (PhDs, MDs, or MBAs in their respective fields). To match these candidates with roles, we evaluate their complex professional experiences and skill sets in comparison with ever-changing leadership roles. It is in and of itself a fascinating challenge. It is why I was drawn to recruiting in the first place.

Normally, hiring is a three-way partnership between the hiring manager, the talent acquisition partner, and the human resource business partner. Because these three work so closely in the hiring process, my book is meant to be shared with anyone within this partnership. In order to have successful hiring, there must be input from all three roles on topics such as job ladder adjustment, internal equity, new job design, career development, offer presentation practices, and, of course, compensation. It is important that the personnel in all three roles communicate with each other effectively at the outset.

The hiring manager in particular must set up a hiring goal, including the timeline to fill the position, and share that with the recruiting team. The more specific the thoughts you share with your recruiting partner are, the better they will understand your goals and be aligned with them. Equally important is that the hiring manger provide timely and specific feedback to the recruiting team. Without such feedback, the recruiting team may end up misplacing resources and, even worse, lose out on potential good hires. An active and engaged hiring manager greatly improves the recruiting and hiring process and is often the difference between successful and unsuccessful hiring teams.

One of the key traits of a successful hiring manager is that they like to provide feedback. Even putting in an extra twenty percent of your time reviewing submitted candidates and providing detailed feedback to the recruiting team can yield greatly improved results, not only in terms of shortening the time period it takes to recruit for these roles, but also in terms of getting much better fits. My suggestion is to provide feedback to your recruiting team within two to three business days. You want to maintain a very motivated and informed team so that they continue to meet your recruiting needs as well as their recruiting priorities. Active hiring managers, in terms of feedback and interviewing, simply get much better results.

I have had hiring managers schedule a weekly review meeting with us, and spend time providing detailed feedback on résumés and interviews on a weekly basis. When this happens, I know that the position will be filled in a timely manner. It is a process that keeps everyone on the same track and keeps everyone moving forward to get things done. Having said that, I don't think a weekly recruiting call is necessary. The best hiring managers I work with simply respond quickly to any recruiting-related questions and give specific guidance when things get stuck. They solve problems quickly and thus motivate their team.

Just as it is important that the hiring manager be actively involved in providing direction and feedback to the recruiting team, it is equally important that the hiring manager provide timely and substantive feedback to the interviewers. The interview team must be educated, not only on the requirements of the role they conduct interviews for, but also on information about the company the interviewee may ask. The interview team must be educated on proper interviewing techniques, the types of questions to ask, how to follow up on certain answers, and other aspects of the process. Teaching interviewers these techniques, which are not as natural as many hiring managers tend to think, is also important in shortening the recruiting process and achieving better results.

Training the hiring managers and their team members on how to interview becomes essential when there is a large volume of recruiting involved and the evaluation process requires more consistency. There are many companies that use behavioral interviews to access talent. One great tool is Lominger's Leadership Architect Tools, well-designed behavior questions asked by the team to evaluate different aspects of talents' leadership skills. I used to give hiring managers training on how to use this effectively. If the interviewers are well-trained, they can also better guide the interviewees how to answer these questions to reflect their true strengths.

Once the hiring partnership is properly constructed, then the recruiting process becomes efficient. The recruiting process is at its most effective when it is fluid, nimble, and adaptable. A good hiring team understands its goals, each person's role within the team, how feedback will work and who to expect it from, and how to adapt to meet challenges and seize opportunities. However, to get this point requires practice and preparation.

Taking an example from my own experiences, I am reminded of a midsize pharmaceutical company I worked with that had particularly effective hiring practices. At this company, the recruiting process always scheduled milestones. Specific dates were set up in advance for interviews. Everyone who was part of the process in any way was informed of these dates, including applicants. Second-round interviews were fluid and adaptable, with the team capable of using online or on-site interviews, as necessary, given the needs of a particular candidate. Everyone involved in the process was aware of these goals and actively worked to meet them on a deadline. As a result of this preparation and clear communication, these goals were almost always met on time. More importantly, these goals were met with high-quality hires.

At the outset, communication is necessary and important to a high-functioning team and cannot be overstated. The hiring team should meet regularly to discuss open roles, the ideal qualifications for those roles, profiles of potential candidates, the current state of the business, and any potential recruiting challenges. This is key in order to have all members of the hiring team on the same page. It is therefore important to schedule regular meetings to discuss ongoing challenges and solutions and to have regular follow-ups on those meetings. This philosophy of regular, structured communication informs all the following chapters in this book.

An effective recruiting process not only benefits the hiring team but also creates a memorable journey for the applicants and interviewees. In the long run, it adds great value to the company's branding, making the employer more appealing in the market place. It energizes the applicants when they become employees of the company and sets them up for later success. In short, an effective recruiting process is an architecture that harnesses positive energy to the organization.

Chapter 4 will focus on the process of having an end goal in mind. While this may seem like a simple step, it is in fact more difficult than most hiring managers realize. The obvious end goal is, of course, a successful hire—but what does having a successful hire mean? It means conceptualizing the successful candidate, a successful process, and a successful hiring team. Chapter 4 will discuss the process of envisioning and how to use envisioning to create successful results.

Chapter 5 focuses more acutely on the talent definition process. The first public step in any recruiting process is the job description, but that requires the hiring manager to think both about the definition of the role—a definition that should be worked on with the team the candidate will eventually work with—and a definition of the job requirements. Putting these together and expressing them clearly to potential candidates, and any outside recruiters the team may work with, requires communication with many people within the hiring company, followed by clear communication to the people conducting the candidate search. This chapter will discuss that process.

Chapter 6 focuses on the search process itself. This is the heart of the recruiting process and is an area in which I have particular insight. The war for talent is getting ever more competitive and understanding how to find the hidden talent that most firms are not accessing, or are even aware of, is key to winning that war.

Chapter 7 focuses on the interview and selection process. Many inexperienced people think of interviewing as simply having a conversation. However, interviewing is an art in which what seems like a conversation is actually a process by which the interviewers both acquire the knowledge to determine whether a candidate is a good fit for their firm (and, it should be noted, this may not necessarily mean being a fit for the role the candidate is interviewing for) and communicate why their firm is a good opportunity for the candidate. The interviewer evaluates and sells at the same time and doing this effectively is a skill. Similarly, so is selecting a candidate after an interview. How do you think about the interview that just occurred? How do you determine if the person presented at the interview will be the person that arrives at the job on day one? Understanding how to think about and answer these questions is discussed in Chapter 7.

Chapter 8 focuses on managing the offer process. I cannot count the number of times I have seen a company find a great candidate, lead them through a multiple-round interview process, evaluate them, make the decision to extend an offer, and then fumble at the goal line by improperly managing the offer process or failing to be proactive. Sealing the deal is the focus of Chapter 8.

Chapter 9 focuses on other obstacles commonly encountered in the recruiting process. While many of these concepts will be touched on in the processes and techniques discussed in Chapters 4 through 8, Chapter 9 identifies common pitfalls in the recruiting process and how to deal with those pitfalls.

Nothing is more important to a company than its talent. The people who make up a firm are the heart and soul of that firm. This is especially so in the biopharmaceutical field. Successful biopharmaceutical companies require exceptional talents: talents to deliver and develop products, talents to evaluate those products, talents to manage the regulatory process for those products, talents to handle the process of bringing those products to market, and talents to ultimately market and sell those products.

Finding and acquiring that talent is difficult, and the firms that do so succeed, while firms that fail to find talent do not last long. My goal is to help you manage the talent acquisition process successfully and help your firm to come out on top.

CHAPTER 4

HAVE AN END GOAL IN MIND

Recruiting is a result-oriented, team-based process. Many obstacles will block your path and situations may feel like they are slipping out of control. But, in fact, recruiting is pretty predictable and you can control the outcome. The secret is to envision your goal before you set forth all the steps for recruiting and hiring. The preparation for hiring starts right here.

As Stephen Covey wrote in his book *The 7 Habits of Highly Effective People*, "All things are created twice. There's a mental or first creation, and a physical or second creation to all things." The physical creation at issue in this book is hiring a successful candidate, and that is discussed at length in the chapters that follow. What we want to focus on first here is the mental creation—envisioning a successful talent acquisition and hiring process.

In my career, I had the opportunity to work with many hiring managers, including some in leading companies as well as companies that struggled. This story is about the latter.

Adam was a relatively inexperienced hiring manager who came to me with what I considered to be a particularly difficult position to fill. As a senior medical director working in a fast-growing midsized biotech company, he wanted to find a board-certified medical director of ophthalmology to represent the company's promising ophthalmic surgical products. The position required extensive travel across the country and possibly internationally, and Adam preferred to have this person located in the corporate office in Dallas, Texas. It would likely involve a significant relocation for the type of candidate the company sought and also required a very specific set of experiences and qualifications that were highly sought after. When I presented our research data of these types of talents in the US domestic market and how much they were compensated, as well as the foreseeable possible challenges, I asked Adam the following questions:

1. Are you willing to hire this individual to work from where he is now without relocation?

2. Are you willing to pay above the typical market compensation level to get the ideal candidate?

The answers to both of these questions were not positive. Adam highly preferred the medical director to be in the corporate office because this was where the majority of the internal stakeholders sat. The company had no commercialized product yet and was quite tight on compensation. The right candidate would be someone who would take a leap of faith and join an organization that he believed in.

Honestly, hiring top talent in the biotech industry is extremely competitive because there is an increasing imbalance of talent supply and demand. With booming new technologies in the biopharma space, the demands for senior-level talents are at a record high. However, it takes years of training and experience to "produce" talent like, for example, a qualified medical doctor, not to mention a board-certified one. Even though Adam had an ideal profile of his hire, he had not thought through where successful candidates would be found and how they could be acquired. Despite thinking of possible challenges of recruiting, he had not communicated these challenges with his recruiting, interviewing, and hiring teams. In this case, he has not prepared himself "mentally" for hiring and set himself up for failure.

Preparing for hiring is a creative mental process that both draws on a hiring manager's experience and challenges his way of thinking openly and critically. In the end, the hiring manager is not "producing" talent but (along with their recruiting counterparts) recruiting and attracting them to the companies, bringing the best out of them in the work place. This is a monumental task, but it starts with mental creation, or what we call "envisioning."

There are four steps in effectively envisioning a successful hire. The first step is to talk with people from the team you are ultimately hiring for or people from other groups that will have a close interaction with them. If you are hiring for a medical director on the clinical development team, talk with another medical director or critical staff member, such as a scientist or someone from regulatory affairs, that this new talent will partner with closely. Find out from these people what traits and experiences they think were most important when they came to work here? What are their daily challenges at work? How did their previous employers differ from this environment? Which skills and experience can be learned quickly and which need to be developed prior to joining this company in order to hit the ground running? What inspires them in this workplace?

These questions will help develop more clarity and understanding of the critical competencies and mind-sets new talent should have in order to be successful and add value in the position. It will also provide broader perspectives on how other companies might be attracting or retaining their talents. Understanding the team you hire for will help you develop successful candidates and properly envision the right fit, which is critical for all subsequent efforts.

Step two: envision the ideal candidate. Armed with the information and insight from step one, begin to envision what the proper candidate will look like for this position. What experiences will he or she have? Are there competitors you may want to pull from? Are there other types of experiences that will be important (for example, experiences in hospital, clinical, or university settings)? Can you think of successful hires in the past for similar roles? What were their profiles like? Is there a geographic component to the search? Would a successful candidate be required to work in a specific geographic area? Are you likely to find candidates in that geographic area or will relocation be necessary? Wrack your brain with these questions, wrestle with them, and develop answers. If you do not have answers to these questions, seek out those who do. Most importantly, you must come out of this process with your mental creation—the ideal candidate.

Everyone gets excited about the concept of an "ideal candidate." What I mean by "ideal candidate" here is the best-suited candidate within the realm of reality. This means someone who can give the best of their talent to you and help you grow your team while developing their career. An "ideal candidate" is someone who can bring the company multiples of the investment that the company put into them. They create lasting values for your team and organization.

Step three: envision the ideal recruiting and hiring process. Once you have gone through this mental process of developing the ideal mental candidate, and after you discussed this ideal candidate with your team members, your recruiters, or your HR partners, your job is only halfway done. Now you must envision the ideal process, which includes both recruiting and selection. The process is a shared responsibility between the hiring manager and the recruiter, however, in my opinion, the hiring manager is the one who ultimately defines this process and owns it. No two hiring processes are the same. Each position presents unique challenges and opportunities. Therefore, at the outset, you must begin asking yourself questions about how the candidate recruiting and selection process will work.

You may have past experiences with similar positions, but you should not limit yourself to simply replicating those processes. As time goes on and positions change, the process will likely change accordingly to reflect the priorities at the time and the competition in the talent market.

Therefore, it is good to reflect on those processes and past experiences. How did it go last time you hired for a similar position? Was the search process lengthy? You thought you would hire a new marketing director for a launching product within two months and ended up not hiring the person until six month later, because the first offer was declined. Was the candidate pool shallow? Maybe you only wanted to interview one candidate among five résumés that you received and the person ended up working for another company. Did you find yourself changing the job requirements in order to open up the field of potential candidates? Remember there was a time you had to upgrade a director of regulatory affairs level to a senior director level, because you were advised by your recruiter that no one was willing to make a lateral move in that niche market.

Did you have to raise compensation or other job benefits in order to attract the right candidate? Did you have to seek extra approvals to get that done? Did you have to engage outside recruiters or were you able to handle the search process in-house? Was relocation an issue? Perhaps candidates were unwilling to relocate to your part of the country, as the cost of living was too high. Did candidates provide feedback on the interview process? If so, what was it? What interview questions and processes really helped you differentiate between potential candidates? How many rounds did it take? How smoothly did the offer process go? Is the candidate you ultimately hired still with your company? These are just some of the questions you need to ask yourself as you envision the ideal search process.

This may seem like a lengthy, and perhaps unnecessary, step. After all, this is likely not your first hiring process. Certainly, you feel it is time to just dive in, get the gears in motion, and start putting your teams to work. In my experience, that is simply the wrong approach. The time you spend in the act of mental creation, for both the right candidate and the right hiring process, ends up being paid back massively in the time saved by avoiding presenting and interviewing inappropriate candidates. This envisioning process will also help you avoid a byzantine hiring process that deters potentially excellent candidates, in which great candidates are not discovered due to a poorly developed search strategy, or candidates do not accept offers due to complications in the offer-making process. Time spent in mental creation results in time saved on the physical creation.

The ideal hiring process would suit the best interests of the employer but would also provide a great experience for the applicants and talent in the job market, who in return will advocate for the company to other people. The experience during the hiring process of those who are chosen for the job is one of the critical factors they consider when making their decision to join.

Step four: communicate your mental creation. It is important to share your mental creations with the teams you work with. As I said at the beginning of this chapter, recruiting is a team-based process. The goal of recruiting and hiring is to make the team a better one. By sharing this mental process, you can let your team know your vision, ask for feedback, and consider it when perfecting the process. Sometimes you may encounter resistance from the team when you create a role or when you ask for different skill sets than they would. They may feel that their skills are not being valued or that the new hire may be a direct competitor for their future promotion. Create a culture that embraces collaboration and fairness.

Finding and hiring talent is a collaborative process, but it is just a beginning. Making a stronger and more competitive team is your ultimate goal in hiring. As a hiring manager, be open-minded in listening to your current team as well as your future team members. Listen, absorb, and be thoughtful when you create this ideal candidate picture in mind. In the end, your investment in time and effort will pay off.

CHAPTER 5
DEFINING THE RIGHT TALENT

Once the mental vision is in place, it is time to turn to the next, more concrete step: putting that vision into words in the form of a job description and set of job requirements. This chapter will focus on how to develop these two building blocks in the talent acquisition process.

Many hiring managers overlook the importance of drafting the job descriptions and the job requirements in the talent acquisition process. I have experienced a number of instances in which I was unwilling to share a job description with potential candidates because I knew the description would not attract certain candidates.

For example, the scope of the responsibilities seemed to be a bit narrower than it actually was. Sometimes the description is written too generally and does not give enough information about the uniqueness about the role. The job description is, in fact, the bedrock of any successful recruiting effort. Not only do these documents guide the teams doing the recruiting, but they also advertise what type of job the candidate is applying for and what this new potential opportunity might look like. The job description is their first impression of the role.

Finally, the job qualifications guide the recruiters and the human resources department. A well-written and thorough job description provides guidance to the recruiter as to what this role is about and gives the human resources department a foundation to match it with the right compensation. Conversely, if the job description is poorly written, it inevitably leads to candidates who are poor fits for the role, wasting the time and resources of all parties involved. Additionally, a poor job description can lead to recruiters not contacting candidates who may, in fact, be a good fit or deter candidates from applying or interviewing, especially those who are not actively seeking new opportunities but are attractive hires.

Important first steps in drafting the job description are reviewing prior job descriptions and discussing the position with the team the potential hire will work with. Get feedback from them, so that the job description is accurate, but also make it a discursive process. Do not just settle for the first set of feedback you get from the team; inquire a bit more and have a comprehensive team review of the role and develop perspectives from key stakeholders. Finally, make sure you understand the readers' perspective and how they will review the job description. Are you attracting the type of talent you want to recruit from? Does your job description energize them to apply for your position? Does your job description provide a good picture of what this role is about?

Where possible, be specific. Avoid generic action verbs like "manage," "oversee," or "direct." If there is a specific field you are looking in (for example, IVD) specify that, as opposed to simply saying "medical device." Again, this will weed out unfit candidates and save you time in the long run. Obviously, though, consult with your company to make sure you are not divulging too much. Know what information is kept close to the vest, such as the name of the drug that is still being developed or the timeline of launch.

In drafting the description of the job qualifications, try to be specific. If you need clinical, hospital, or academic experience, say so. If there is a specific prior job title you want, make sure it is in the job description. If you seek a candidate with at least a certain number of years of experience, say as much.

Beyond these specific job qualifications, be sure to set forth the soft skills and personality traits that you look for in a potential hire. For example, a regional sales director role at a biotech company may require strong critical thinking skills in addition to strong leadership experience. He or she needs to be able to look at the business from many different angles and be able to form a competitive strategy for the business as it continues to evolve. Only someone with strong critical thinking skills would be able to do so. Oftentimes, these soft skills and personality traits are treated as an afterthought—something to pad out the job qualifications and make the list appear longer. However, these are helpful to your recruiters when they conduct their initial contact interview. They can get a sense of whether the potential candidate does, in fact, possess these soft skills.

Besides the soft skills, finding the right personality and mentality is equally important, if not more so, as the right experience, because these things are hard to change and develop compared to skills. Your job is to be a conduit that takes the information about what type of co-worker the team is looking for, provided by those who will ultimately work with the candidate, to the recruiting team doing the first pass at searching and screening. An accurate and fulsome description allows that searching and screening to be as focused as possible.

Also important is discussing the job description and job qualifications with your recruiting team or outside recruiting partner. It may not be clear on paper which aspects of the job and qualifications are the most important. For example, when a certain experience is highly preferred, such as "FDA submission experience in a rare diseases area," do you give consideration to other experiences and, if so, what type of experiences would those be? A conversation with the recruiting team or outside recruiting firm can make that clear and allow for more accurate searching and screening. When you meet with the recruiter, take the opportunity to ask them questions about their perspective on the talent market. From their recruiting experience, how challenging or realistic is it to find people with such skill sets? Does the title reflect the seniority of the skill sets and experience it requires? Would it attract the right talent to apply for the role?

Ultimately, the output of a search and screening process is only as good as the input. While an experienced recruiting team can streamline the search and screening process greatly, if that team is provided with vague or inaccurate job descriptions and lists of job qualifications, their job becomes more difficult and the process becomes lengthier and more costly. Spending the time to make the job descriptions and list of job qualifications as thorough as possible will benefit the process immensely.

Consider the job description and list of job qualifications from the candidate's perspective as well. These documents will be among the first things the candidate receives and they play an important role in self-screening. The job description and list of qualifications can communicate to the potential candidate a great deal about company culture. What traits are valued? What is the team ultimately like? Company culture and reputation are among the leading factors determining whether or not a candidate makes a decision to accept a role. This is a chance to tell the potential client about company culture and begin selling them on becoming a hire.

A good example of this would be clearly describing the scope of responsibilities, both strategically and tactically, to give the candidate a good idea of what the position is about. Regarding the requirements, it's very important to differentiate required experience, highly preferred experience, and preferred experience, as well as if any alternative experience is possible. For example, if a candidate does not have highly preferred experience such as "infectious diseases," would the hiring manager consider "inflammation" experience? If so, then this should be used as alternative listed on the job description. If a degree in biological science is highly preferred but not required, list a few other majors on the job description or be clear that this degree is preferred but not required.

One recent trend I have seen in the recruiting process is for hiring managers to include a short biography about themselves in the job description. This makes the job description more personal and becomes an added selling point to potential candidates. I think it is a great idea and a wonderful opportunity to sell the candidate on your firm. Communicating culture is difficult but vital. As a hiring manager, you should take every opportunity to communicate what sets your firm apart from competitors and makes it an ideal place to work.

Another thought is to include short bios of the candidate's potential teammates, helping candidates get a feel for the team. Not only is this a great selling point that will help you stand out from the competitors for talent, but it will also aid in screening. It is just as helpful to have potential candidates envision a team they feel they would be a great fit on as it is for them to self-screen away from a team on which they may not be a good fit.

I have attended numerous intake calls with hiring managers with the job description presented to me at the intake. It is interesting that more than half of the time hiring managers ask me if I have any questions to ask first, before they share with me anything about their team and the position. These were hiring managers I had never worked with before, and I didn't know much about their personality, team, business, or culture. My assumption as to why this happens so often is that hiring managers often expect recruiters to understand the role from the job description itself, because we are the "experts." These hiring managers are also very seasoned senior level professionals and they have been with the hiring company for many years. It takes a mind-set shift for them to look at their team, business, and culture from an outside-in approach. Though I normally do extensive research before a meeting, it is essential to gain insight from the hiring manager directly before any recruiting efforts take place.

This observation also makes me believe that, if a hiring manager wants to make a successful hire, they need to always think from the talent's perspective. How are the company and the team reviewed from outside? How are my leadership skills viewed? Do I share that passion when I hire people to work for me? Essentially, recruiting is a two-way process. The top talent is interviewing and selecting companies and hiring managers too.

Looking back on my career, I can see many examples of how hiring processes played out in practice. For example, I once worked with a hiring manager who was a vice president of commercial development, who led the global sales and marketing team at a large size biopharma company. He wanted to hire a global director of portfolio to manage their leading medical device portfolio. We discussed the role, and he set forth very few criteria for the candidate, as he wanted to be open and see more candidates who had leadership potential. He didn't limit his range of candidates to any specific product category other than the IVD industry, nor did he limit his candidates to certain company background. This made our target profile extremely vague. I knew he must have had an ideal profile in mind, but he just didn't want to confine the search to certain experience as he knew the talent pool was already too small.

So, my next step was to study the profiles of all the members of the current team. Perhaps this would give me insight into what the culture of the team was like, what personality traits were valued, and what seniority level would make for a successful hire. After having had a chance to complete my investigation, I then had a follow-up call with the hiring manager and his direct report. We discussed my observations about team composition and what I thought would be a good fit with the team. I gathered the following: his team members were largely from a few major competitors. They all had around fifteen to twenty years of progressive experience in the medical device field at the director level. They had all attended top schools and worked for well-known companies. Therefore, someone who was going to be their peer at the same level would hold similar qualifications, but the hiring manager may prefer to add diversity to complement the team.

For example, I suggested someone from a more nimble and robust smaller biotech company and someone who has strong scientific, opposed to business, background. The individual needed to have an impressive leadership track record to be able to establish credibility and potentially grow to lead other team members as part of the succession plan, as this hiring manager ideally expected.

The hiring manager heard me and provided his feedback on my observations and thoughts. Based on my investigation, his feedback, our discussions, and my own sense of the hiring manager from this process, I crafted what I felt was an accurate list of qualifications to guide us in sourcing and recruiting efforts. I also anticipated that the hiring manager would put a lot of emphasis on leadership skills, so we engaged a leadership assessment partner to be part of our recruiting process so that we could present candidates as well as a scientific report on the candidate's leadership evaluation.

Within a week, we had four strong, local candidates. They were presented to the interviewing team, and after a four-week interview process, there was a successful hire. While not all hiring processes will go this smoothly, it was clear that the extra effort I put in to determining more about the right candidate and drafting an accurate and truly descriptive job description and lists of job qualifications led to a process where we talked to the right candidates and the candidates were self-selected properly. The candidate who went through the entire process not only was a great fit in terms of skills and culture but also was fully engaged and committed to the process, as she felt this was also a rare opportunity for her.

I credit the success of such hiring to the accurate description of an ideal candidate. Though the job description started seemingly vague, thorough, detailed discussion with the hiring team and research done by the recruiting team had almost drawn a picture of what this talent would be like and validated that hiring such talent could be done in an effective manner. This process itself provides further clarity on why the talent is desired on the team, what is expected, and how they can be further developed. This is what I like about recruiting—it is always a win-win between talents and employers.

Just as it is important to develop a clear mental image of the right candidate and the right process, it is important to put that image to paper and discuss what exactly the ideal candidate looks like. As a hiring manager, continue to raise the bar of the talent you are hiring, but do not always measure candidates by experience. The intangibles, such as motivation, passion, collaborative mentality, learning agility, commitment to grow with team, and interest in developing other team members are invaluable to your team as well. These traits are not only hard to measure but also rare. Spend time thinking about how you define a top candidate by identifying these traits and recruiting these people to your team. Once you do, you will find this process will pay off immensely and create lasting value for your team and the company.

CHAPTER 6
SEARCH RELENTLESSLY

The question that bedevils all hiring managers is how do you find the right candidates? You and your competitors are all looking at the similar candidates and trying to fill similar roles. So how do you find the hidden talent—the candidates your competitors overlook? How do you find the best talent that suits your organization's needs quickly so that they come on board sooner, keeping you a step ahead of your competitors? Learning to find these candidates is the focus of this chapter.

Recruiting is an all-or-nothing business. You either find the right candidate and your company grows, or you spend resources while leaving a job unfilled or, even worse, fill it with the wrong person. This is what I love about recruiting. It is a very measurable and highly competitive business. A successful search process is a relentless one.

The key here is quite simple—you need to run an *expansive* search. Search everyone everywhere and tap deeply into the top talent pool. You must do this in the most efficient manner, which means searching quickly for the best-quality candidates. Ordinarily, searches are conducted relying on candidate applications supplied through an online job portal or a recruiting database that may have been developed through past applicants, the recruiting team's personal experiences, or the recruiting team's network. However, this is not sufficient for a relentless search methodology.

How do we define relentless?

Relentless means never give up and never say no. Never accept anything less than what you really wanted. Aim high and hold yourself to that standard. When it comes to searching for talent, relentless searching is guided by the ideal candidate profile you have in mind and the talent strategy you set forth for your team. Keep searching extensively until you find the talent you desire.

As a specialized executive search agency, our search process may be very different from that of a corporate recruiting team. This is because when a client engages us on a talent search, we know already this role does not generate active job applicants and our client has been recruiting for some time without any success.

We start with an extensive industry search of competitors, key players, notable conferences, keynote speakers, industry experts, etc. Then we take all that information to form a robust search strategy, as well as a sourcing process supported by cutting edge recruiting technologies.

What are the two key components to guarantee a relentless search process consistently?

The first key component is to develop a sourcing system and then test it, tweak it, and make it perfect over time. We refer to this as a relentless search process. The main characteristics of a relentless search process are:

- identifying the majority of hidden talent from the talent market
- engaging with these talents in a consultative career discussion so that they reveal their true selves and we can do a good matchmaking.

The second key component is to implement this system using a high-performing recruiting team who is both experienced and process driven so that the process consistent.

The tools most recruiters use include but are not limited to LinkedIn, company websites, various talent or industry contact databases, and social media platforms. Take LinkedIn for example. As executive search recruiters, LinkedIn is one of our best friends at work. We work with it on a daily basis. In my entire career, I have known fewer than ten people who do not have a LinkedIn profile. On LinkedIn's recruiter page, we can conduct extensive industry searches on competitors, size of the companies, total number of talent in particular industry segment, and job mobility in a given period or a given location. You can develop key search terms, communicate them with your recruiting team, and have your recruiting team return with as many candidates as possible. This is where your list of job qualifications comes into play. Hopefully you have developed a detailed list that allows your search team to limit results while searching boldly to find only those who are truly potential fits for your organization. If your search team is bringing back too many results, that is a sign that you need to refine your search terms or develop more search terms.

Also, be clear about the geographic scope of your search. Should your recruiters be confined to a certain area? Should they search in the radius of a key city or is this a nationwide search with the possibility of relocation funding? Let your search team know these things upfront.

Another helpful search technique is to run a broader search upfront that lets you know the size of the overall pool of candidates you are looking at. You may want to know, for example, how many directors of regulatory affairs there are in the medical device industry. Knowing these facts can help you determine how specific to make your search terms. It is important to get a sense of how deep your search pool is to let you know if you need to consider candidates with less, or alternative, experience. Do not be afraid to revisit your mental picture.

Another approach to consider in directing your search team is whether there are experiences other than working for biopharmaceutical companies that may be useful for a particular role. For example, experience in a hospital may be transferrable to a commercial-based clinical setting. Talent working in the management consulting industry may be transitioned into biopharma industry to work as an in-house consultant.

Another consideration is people who may work in similar positions in related fields. You need not compromise your vision, but you also need to question your initial thoughts if the talent pool simply is not deep enough. One of my first recruiting assignments that I got from a client when I started Bongene Search was to recruit for a chemist. The hiring manager was very particular about his talent knowing this one lab system; however, the final hire, whom our client was so excited about, did not have the system knowledge. But she demonstrated very strong learning ability and other great skills needed to be successful on the job.

Relocation is always an important consideration, especially if you seek to attract hard-to-find talent in a specialized role. In my experience, potential candidates are more open than ever to the idea of relocation. There simply needs to be a proper relocation package and an understanding of the disruptions that may come with relocation. I would certainly encourage you to direct your search team to be expansive in its geographic search to find the best fit. Almost all the searches we conduct these days are drawn from a nationwide talent pool. Geography mobility is also a requirement to develop senior leadership within the company—not only domestically, but sometimes globally.

Another great resource is leading conferences in the field. Your search teams should be on Google, searching for annual leading conferences and their participants and keynote speakers. These conferences are normally serving the key players in the industry and top talent that your competitors are retaining.

Though LinkedIn is a great research and professional tool, it is not perfect. Talent may not update their profiles on LinkedIn or they may not be active on it. The point is to utilize it to search but never to rely on it. Search tools should be multiple, and they should complement one another. The only way to find passive candidates is through more hard-targeted searches, and do it consistently and integrate all pieces together. For example, you may find a top-notch oncology MD's name from a recent paper he published, but you do not have his contact info yet. You can take the info and search in LinkedIn, find the email address there, and send him a message, or maybe you can contact him through a mutual network that you belong to.

Passive candidates are considered passive applicants. However, do not believe for a moment that simply because a candidate is passive they will not be open to the right opportunity. I have had conversations countless times with candidates who, though they were not actively in the job market, only needed to hear about the right opportunity to begin thinking about making a move. Even hiring managers sometimes ask us to keep them in mind for career opportunities. For ethical reasons we do not recruit our hiring managers to other companies when we have a contract to work for that client. However, it does say that everyone is looking or at least would be willing to listen to new career opportunities. This is what makes recruiting so competitive all the time. Identifying and reaching out to these passive candidates is an essential part of any search process. Again, the search process must be relentless, process-driven, and carried out by highly skilled and trained recruiters.

In my own firm, since our search starts with research about the entire industry, we always set forth on the right path and aim to include as many qualified candidates as possible. Through our thorough research, we define a total talent pool of candidates for a particular position. Using our own proprietary search techniques, we build connections and relationships with as many candidates as possible in a particular field. Many of these great talents are nurtured by us over many years. Sometimes, candidates who may not be a good fit for one position turn out to be a great fit for another position down the line, but we do not give up until we find candidates with the proper fit. In our business, we strive for a 1:1 candidate-to-interview ratio, while other agencies typically yield 1:4 or greater. At Bongene Search, we expect that the candidates we present will be candidates the hiring team wants to interview.

As examples of our search process, I would like to focus on a couple searches we ran in the past. Once, we were given an assignment to hire four PhD-level bioinformatics scientists for a major biotechnology company. The company sought candidates with infectious disease experience. Within two weeks, we had mapped out over 5,000 PhD-level bioinformatics scientists across the United States with one to three years of professional experience. We then contacted and screened those potential candidates regarding their NGS (next-generation sequencing) experience and their therapeutic experience in the clinical setting. By the end of the search process, we had filled three of the four positions, and the only position we did not fill went to an internal candidate at that time.

We were able to effectively hire the best talent for our client because we almost dominated the entire US talent market in this field. We always do that and leave no chance that we cannot fill the position with a right candidate.

Similarly, with regards to a particular position, such as a director of sales or sales manager role, we would map out an average of 500-1000 candidates in the local market. We then screen those talents and begin our pre-interviewing process. For higher-level positions, such as a managing director of oncology, we would similarly map out all the potential candidates in the area with the relevant skill sets and background and begin engaging immediately. Our goal is to uncover hidden talent in the most efficient manner while at the same time advising hiring managers on what types of candidates they may want to look for and whom we can bring forward in the process, keeping the top talent engaged in the hiring process.

At the end of the day, a successful search process is about having a vision of what you want out of successful candidate, having flexibility and adaptability to allow you to consider outside-the-box approaches to identifying candidates, and having the tenacity to identify the pool of both active and passive candidates.

When you think about it, the past three chapters are interconnected. Having an end goal in mind means the right talent can be identified and recruited, no matter what it takes, but you can only achieve this by implementing a relentless search process and having a relentless mind-set. Hiring an external recruiting firm, such as the one I created, that is laser-focused on perfecting the recruiting craft, will generate the best results.

CHAPTER 7
INTERVIEW AND SELECT INTELLIGENTLY

A fter a relentless search process, normally taking place over two to four weeks, we typically have five to ten candidates to present on a rolling basis. The interview and selection process can commence at this point.

The selection process is the heart of hiring. Once you identify interested candidates based on your mental model of the ideal candidate, you need to make sure those candidates are the right fit. Traditionally, this has been done through an interview process, sometimes consisting of multiple rounds. The traditional model is to essentially hold conversations and then have each person on the interview team evaluate the candidate based on their impressions of that conversation. Oftentimes, there are levels of screening, some with more senior personnel reserved for candidates who have already been vetted in some way.

While that traditional model makes sense intuitively, there are subtle tweaks you can make to the interview and evaluation process that result in a better selection of candidates. Employing these principles and approaches can avoid the twin problems of wasting valuable staff time interviewing candidates who are not a good fit while ensuring that candidates who may be good fits are not weeded out prematurely.

The first important consideration is the interview team. When considering the formation of the interview team, you should consider factors such as:

- Will this interviewer work with the eventual hire?
- Does this interviewer work regularly with the team for which I'm hiring?
- How engaged will this interviewer be in the interview process? Unfortunately, there are just some personnel who view the task of interviewing as a distraction from other aspects of their work. Obviously, this will color their approach to the interview process.
- Is this interviewer a good salesman for my firm? The interview is as much about selling the firm to the potential hire as it is about evaluating the

potential hire. You need to select interviewers who will be salesmen.

- Am I including interviewers from varying levels of seniority? It is important that the evaluation process have input from both junior and senior members of your organization. Senior members have a wealth of past experiences to draw on and may take have a more long-term view of hiring. Junior members have been in the job market more recently may have a better read on qualifications and can also help avoid some generational bias.

- Is my interviewing panel diverse? Inclusivity is important, and you do not want to send the wrong message about your firm by creating an interview panel that lacks diversity.

If you have control over the composition of your interviewing team, consider these factors and try to develop a strong, diverse team.

Scheduling the interview process is also important. How many rounds will the process be? Typically there should be no more than three rounds of on-site interviews. For phone interviews, it would be fine to have three or more. How far apart will these rounds be scheduled? What time will be set aside for debriefing and evaluating potential candidates? Will there be a mix of phone and live interviews? At what point are more senior personnel, whose time may be scarce, going to be participating? Once you have this schedule, be sure it is communicated to and confirmed with all the necessary participants.

The first step is ordinarily a pre-screening interview. This is usually conducted by your in-house recruiting team or your outside recruiting partner. This is where the job description and list of job qualifications described previously becomes important. These tools are what your recruiter will use to evaluate whether it makes sense to move a candidate forward to an interview with the hiring team. Again, it is crucial that these tools be accurate and comprehensive in order to allow the recruiter to properly vet potential candidates and avoid wasting company time on candidates who are clearly not a good fit.

At the pre-screening stage, select the candidates who both meet the minimum qualifications and leave a good impression with their energy level and how much research they have done about your company. These two aspects indicate their true interest in a role and how much initiative they normally take to pursue a role. I've partnered some senior executives who are great people readers. They told me they primarily assess a talent these days by their energy level and if it is synced with their team environment. It always turns out to be a reliable predictor of actual enthusiasm for a role.

The next step is usually to move the candidate on to a hiring team interview. The hiring team usually consists of hiring managers or other human resource personnel, members of the team the candidate will work with, and other key stakeholders, such as team managers. This stage usually consists of multiple rounds of interviews, some of which may take place over the phone or live in person. It is important to remember, especially once a candidate reaches the live interview rounds, that the interview process is as much about selling your firm to the candidate as it is about evaluating the candidate. Keep this in mind as you design your process and select your interviewing team. It is also important to have some flexibility built into your interview process. It could be to accommodate the candidate's busy schedule—maybe he can only do a remote interview in the coming weeks. If that's the case, you can do the digital interview first and evaluate. It could also mean that instead of having a formal office interview, you can invite the candidate to an off-work setting, like a coffee shop, to have a more casual meeting to learn about one another.

An effective interview team is approximately eight to ten people. If you use fewer than that, you may not gather enough information to make an effective decision on a candidate. Alternatively, employing more than eight interviewers can make for a tedious interviewing process, which can turn off the candidate. Too many interviewers would also make for a confusing experience, with too many people providing repetitive or conflicting input. I have seen interview processes that have included as many as fifteen interviewers. Those were not effective processes. It dragged on too long, took up too much time for everyone involved, and in the end created a paralysis of analysis, as too many opinions about candidates had to be sifted through. Having too many interviewers also creates scheduling nightmares.

In my experience, any particular round of interviewing should not consist of any more than four interviewers. Again, more than that creates a tedious process for all involved. Also, interview fatigue can set in, and if interviews are conducted later in the day, interviewers may not see the potential candidate in their best or most representative state.

It should also be clear to each interviewer what their role is in the process. Assign them particular personality traits, qualifications, or experiences to look for. One interviewer may focus on a candidate's educational background, while another may focus on times the candidate has demonstrated a particular soft skill, such as leadership, or familiarity with a particular aspect of their work assignment, such as approval of cancer drugs by the Food and Drug Administration. By assigning these tasks, the hiring manager can avoid redundant questions and prevent any one interviewer from hijacking the interview process. Additionally, if there are any questions you do not want asked, either generally or to a specific candidate, make it clear to the interview team.

Decide on backup interviewers as well. Unscheduled issues arise that prevent people from interviewing, and you do not want to the interviewing process derailed because something arose that prevented an interviewer from participating. Be considerate of the candidate's time by being prepared for this. I have seen situations where firms have lost out on very good candidates because reshuffling the interview schedule caused the candidate to lose interest in the interview process.

There are a variety of interview styles and forms to choose from. Phone interviews, web interviews, and of course, the standard in-person interview are all employed. In regards to recruiting for senior-level positions, I have noticed recently that increasingly, firms use web interviews for the first stage of the process and then move on to informal in-person interviews that may take place at an outside location, such as a coffee shop. While this would seem like a major departure from the usual formal interviewing process, there is a logic behind it. At the senior level, culture fit is of utmost importance. For better or worse, senior-level candidates are fairly set in their ways and finding senior-level staff who fit within the culture of the firm is often difficult. Firms find it easier to evaluate a cultural fit in informal settings.

New hires are most successful when they bond with the culture of the team or the company. The clients I have worked with all have many different cultures. Some of them are more focused on corporate values like stability and have quite a long chain of command, while others are fast growing medium- sized firms that tend to be very nimble. They are still unknown to most of the talent out there, but they make decisions very quickly. The mentalities required for these two types of companies would be very different.

The use of web and phone interviews is also a convenient way to deal with last-minute hiccups. Emergencies do happen, on both the hiring team side and candidate side, so web and phone interviews are convenient ways to deal with those emergencies while staying on a set interview schedule. Use technology to stay on your interviewing timeline. Flexibility is key to any successful interviewing process.

The Interview Process

Read the Résumé Thoroughly—
It Tells a Lot about a Person's Style

What about interviewing skills themselves? First and foremost, be sure to set aside ample time to read and consider both résumés and any notes provided by the initial recruiter, and make sure your interview team does the same. Understand the candidate before finalizing the interview process. I've spoken with candidates countless times who knew that their interviewers were reading their résumé for the first time only at the interview. You can see the interviewer scan the résumé and then just pick out particular experiences or job titles that catch their eye. For most candidates, this is a red flag. It shows that the interviewing firm has not really considered candidates closely, and in an intensely competitive talent market, that can certainly be enough to deter a candidate from choosing your firm. Know the candidates' résumés and have the areas you want to ask questions about highlighted before you walk in the room. Instruct your other interviewers to do the same.

Have End Goals in Mind and Design Interview Questions to Evaluate Both Hard and Soft Skills

Have end goals in mind when you conduct an interview. The interview should not be a scattered conversation. What are the interesting experiences you want to know more about? What are the concerns or gaps in a candidate's résumé that you want to explore further? Know the answers to these questions and have, at the very least, a mental outline of where you see the conversation going and what you hope to learn. Similarly, think about any soft skills you hope to learn about in this interview and design interview questions that will effectively explore those soft skills.

Effective interviewers are able to balance two competing concerns. On the one hand, the interviewers have their goals in mind at the outset and develop a mental map of how to meet those goals through the interview process. On the other hand, they are good listeners. They are able to process the responses the candidate provides and transform those answers into quality follow-up questions. One role you may want to assign, if you have a team of interviewers, is a listener and have that person solely ask follow-up questions. In the end, this is a skill—being both a conversation leader and follower—built through practice and you will get a sense of what works for you by conducting interviews.

I also recommend an interview approach focused on behavioral questions. Ask how candidates have handled particular work situations in the past. These questions can be granular, such as asking about how candidates have dealt with a very specific work scenario they are likely to encounter in the position for which they interview, or these questions can be more open-ended to see if the candidate has certain requisite personality traits. In the end, the résumé tells you much of what you need to know about a candidate's experiences and qualifications. The interview is your opportunity to learn about soft skills, general abilities (including communication), and personality. You will also learn a great deal about the level of preparation a candidate puts into the interview, which may give you information about whether the candidate is truly the right hire.

Below are my top-five behavior questions to ask talents:

- What is your biggest accomplishment in your career and why?
- What was a time you solved a major issue with your team?
- What was a time when you had to made a quick decision or take an immediate action when you were not given clear direction? What was the result?
- What was a time when you had to confront your manager or someone whose status was higher than you?
- Tell me about a time you had to learn something quickly.

Through the preparation of these types of behavior questions with our talent, I always find the ones who got the final offer in the end were not the ones who answered the question the most effectively the first time, but the ones who had the best attitude and who were most patient, provided specific information, and answered these questions in a clear, logical way. Maybe their styles are not the most compelling, but you can tell the replies have substance and they are very sincere in making their points. Once I provide some feedback on their style or to the structure they should answer in, they always impress the hiring manager and interview quite successfully.

Conducting the interview is a systematic approach on the hiring team side. I would coordinate with the hiring team about what types of behavioral questions each member of the hiring team should ask. Having set roles is key to the success of this approach. Assign note-taking responsibilities as well, with each team member looking for certain personality traits within the interview. For example, one member of the interview team may be tasked with considering how confidently a candidate was able to discuss leadership experiences. Another could be tasked with evaluating how collaborative a candidate seems. Energy levels and body language are all things you should instruct your interview team to pay attention to. Your interviewers will become better listeners if you give their listening focus. They also then do not feel that they are asking repetitive questions again and again. The candidates will feel much more respected and valued if the interview is a well-designed and structured team process. They will easily gain different perspectives and insights into the company and form a more rounded impression of the team when each team member's role in the interview process is clearly defined.

Debriefing

Almost as important as the interview process is the interview debriefing process. The debriefing session should be established at the same time as the interview, so that no team member can delay participation for other obligations. Ideally, the debriefing session should occur within one to three business days of the interview, while the interviewers' memories of it are still fresh. Interviewers should consult their notes and conduct the debriefing session in-person or over the phone. The best practice is to send a reminder of expectations for the debriefing session prior to the session. You may also want to remind interviewers what their particular role was during the interview.

Reaching consensus while debriefing is not easy and may not even be necessary. Every interviewer will come to the debriefing session with a different perspective, personality, and their own style. The hiring manager should try to categorize each interviewer's feedback into one of three categories: "recommend," "not recommend," or "neutral." Red flags that have been noted by particular interviewers should be discussed in detail. Remember that your role during the debriefing session should be that of facilitator, helping each interviewer articulate their view. Also be careful not to let particular interviewers dominate the feedback session. In any group, some people will tend to try talk over others. Some candidates will elicit particularly strong responses from particular interviewers.

Keep the conversation flowing and allow everyone to participate. The point is for you to have as much feedback as possible when you make your decision. This is best accomplished by creating a feedback process in which every interviewer feels welcome to participate, does so, and then comes to a definitive landing on how they feel about the candidate. However, in the end, the decision to hire, or recommend hire, will be in your hands. Make sure you feel like you have the information you need to make that decision.

Selecting a candidate for a role is a complex process. Most companies form a decision after several phone and on-site interviews. Sometimes, decisions are made after only one or two conversations. Other evaluation tools, especially when hiring senior-level talent or talent for roles in which leadership skills are of importance, may also be useful.

Selection

Talent Assessment by Hiring Manager

There are many companies who focus on talent assessment, such as by testing for sales or leadership skills. We work with our clients to integrate their assessment partners into the selection process. Take sales, for example—a few of our clients ask applicants to take an online test before they proceed with an interview. They believe the test to be a good indicator for future success. But nothing is absolute. More than anything else, the assessment test provides hiring managers a consistent tool to evaluate different applicants and gives them reassurance in their decision so they can focus their energy and attention elsewhere.

I partnered with a hiring manager who was quite indecisive about a candidate whom I felt very strongly about. What he was reluctant on was her personality. He was not sure if she was indeed an extrovert, a go-getter. After learning of this issue, we partnered with a reputable assessment company that focuses on evaluating personalities. When the report came out, it showed that she was an extremely extroverted person and was extremely driven by goals. It gave the hiring manager tremendous confidence to move her to the next stage in the process, which resulted in hiring her in the end.

Candidate's Perspective

Finally, be sure to consider your talent evaluation process from the candidate's perspective. Be thoughtful when you ask questions and make sure your interviewing team is as well. It should never appear that you and your team are simply going through a checklist; it should be apparent to the candidate that the candidate's experiences and qualifications are getting thorough consideration. Show passion, warmth, and interest. Make sure the candidate has ample time to ask questions as well. Not only is this important to take care of any potential concerns the candidate may have about your organization, but it also allows you to see whether the candidate has taken the time to develop well-considered questions about your organization, which is an important evaluation tool. A candidate who has not thought of good questions is not a prepared candidate.

Be thoughtful about the candidate's personal concerns as well. Listen to them about scheduling and travel concerns. Provide lunch! Allowing members of your evaluation team to have lunch with a candidate is a great opportunity to learn more about the candidate in a casual setting. The candidate may be more open about themselves, or red flags that would not emerge in a formal interview setting may show themselves during lunch. Be thoughtful when sending over the interview confirmation packet. The candidate is evaluating your firm as well, so put your best foot forward from the outset. A typo in the interview confirmation packet, for example, may indicate to a candidate that this a firm does not take professionalism seriously. Make sure candidates have adequate office directions so they do not have to rely on Google Maps or a GPS. Be sure to greet them at the lobby and escort them through your building. Give the candidate's timely feedback, even if you are not going forward with them. As interviewing and selection are two-way streets, make the experience a high priority.

Why Is a Candidate's Experience So Important?

First of all, it helps the company build a healthy brand and thus creates lasting brand loyalty. People talk about their interview experiences, and they use the interview to network and learn about the company. If they are not happy with certain things they experience or see, they will talk about it with other people.

A positive candidate experience normally means a well-designed, personalized interview experience, which is a reflection of the well-being of the company's business strategy and its link to talent acquisition. Normally this type of company would hire talent fast and attract better talent, and thus increase its bottom line.

A positive candidate experience also boosts a company's current employees' morale and increases employee retention and productivity. If a company treats its potential employees with respect and care, it gives its current employees more of these benefits.

Last but not least, a positive candidate experience generates more referrals and makes hiring faster, so the company is filled with better-quality candidates who are attracted to work with it.

The candidate's experience is one of the most invisible competitive edges in the talent war. You select talent, and at the same time, you are being evaluated and selected. Make sure you design the interview and selection process to provide the most positive experience. This normally means:

- Clear communication through the job description and keeping communication open through the entire interview process, including providing feedback to candidates.

- Shorter interview times and fewer layers of communication to the hiring manager when the candidate tries to learn more about their future manager and team culture.

- Willingness to personalize the interview process to accommodate flexibility and add personal touches during the interview process

- Treating each candidate as a customer with respect and care, rather than a job applicant who comes for an interview and needs to be hired.

- Developing a long relationship with candidates who showed interest in your company and engaging them in a future communication by digital media

To recap, the interview and selection process functions best when it is unbiased, collaborative, flexible, reliable, and mutual. Once this process is completed, a talent is identified and will move to the next step in the process—the offer stage.

CHAPTER 8

MANAGE THE OFFER
PROCESS PROACTIVELY

I have seen so many hiring managers carry out a thorough recruiting, interview, and selection process, only to have the perfect candidate slip through their fingers due to improperly managing the job offer process. Avoiding that last-second fumble is the subject of this chapter.

Not only is the offer stage a collaborative process among the hiring manager, the recruiting partner, and the HR business partner, but it also engages with and involves the selected talent. As we discussed in earlier chapters, we envision that all things have happened in the process and then manage it backward. It requires a very proactive thinking process and a thoughtful approach to address any possible challenges and pitfalls.

The key word in a successful offer management process is "communication." As a hiring manager, you must communicate with the candidate directly. Do not think this is something that's just taken care of by your recruiter or HR partner. Your direct communication with the selected candidate engages them in this final critical stage. While a recruiter or HR's job is to keep the candidate informed on where the selection process is at the moment, you can continue to share your interest in working with them through a quick email or phone call. This normally happens after the decision is made but before the offer is extended. Stay in touch with your candidates, no matter what. Let them feel you are accessible and supportive.

We recently hired a director of commercial development for a client. The hiring manager and the candidate developed a great rapport during the process. After the interview, the hiring manager left a thank-you message to the candidate over the phone, thanking her for spending two days with them and traveling for the interview. In the message, she also revealed that the interview went well and that she had a strong interest in hiring her. The candidate got the message immediately when she landed at her local airport after traveling for five hours. She was completely blown away and touched by the passion the hiring manager had for the business, as well as the trust and belief the hiring manager had developed in her. She told me that if she got the offer, she would like to work with this hiring manager.

The next day, an offer was extended. Though the candidate negotiated a bit with regards to compensation, she happily accepted the position the same day the offer was revised, which was so pleasant. The company saved almost a week's time by hiring her sooner and kept the hire very energetic and motivated. All these great things happened because the hiring manager was committed to acquiring a great talent.

Meanwhile, the recruiting partner, whether internal or external, continues to play a role in engaging the candidate in the process until the position is officially closed. This may include providing interview feedback or creating the timeline needed to make a hiring decision or the timeline to extend an offer. Even if the company decides not to extend an offer to a pool of candidates, a communication of the interview status and decision should always take place to provide a positive interview experience to talent.

When communicating with candidates who finished the interview process, you will always gain additional information about the interview or feedback from their perspective. They may share with you what other opportunities are like or what the interview style was of a particular team member. This is all great information and, if utilized well, can improve your interview process and make your company brand stronger.

In follow-up conversations, it is important to gauge the candidate's level of interest in the position. Usually, hiring managers manage multiple candidates for a position at once. The follow-up conversations are opportunities to evaluate which candidates seem truly interested in the position while keeping the others engaged. Ask open-ended questions about their impression of the company or the role and encourage them to ask any questions relative to this role or the team.

Through their reply, you can develop an accurate judgment whether the candidate is still highly interested. Besides, as the interviews will likely be finished at this point, they might be more open to reveal their thoughts, which gives the hiring manager an opportunity to further assess if they are a good cultural fit.

Surprisingly, many companies fail to take this important step. They do little to gauge the candidate's level of interest or to keep the candidate interested, only interacting with the candidate when they follow-up themselves or when they enter the next official step in the selection process. Needless to say, this is not the best practice, and I have seen companies lose great candidates due to lack of follow-up.

These follow-up conversations are also useful opportunities to obtain candidate expectations about things such as compensation and benefits. It's also a great opportunity to learn about a candidate's current compensation, if that has not been disclosed previously. Most likely at this stage, you design your offer package for the candidate you are interested in hiring. Knowledge is power as you enter those negotiations. Use this time to gather the information you need.

Designing and making the actual offer to a candidate is an extremely complex process that requires considering many factors and the approval of a number of stakeholders. It is not uncommon for a job offer to take up to one month to get final approval. Of course, the quicker the process moves along, the better. Candidates do not like to be strung along. Likely, candidates already have a current employer and are considering other offers. The laggards in this race are not the winners. Therefore, the quicker you can move along the approval process, the better.

Keep up momentum by being in contact with the key staff within your organization and with the candidate. Be as candid with the candidate as possible. You may want to tell the backup candidate directly that there is one candidate leading the process and a final decision has not been made yet. You should have an answer for them within two weeks. Do share your timeline so that the talent may follow up with you directly based on the timeline. Talent understands that the hiring manager normally interviews a few candidates and similarly, the candidate also pursues multiple opportunities at once. Candidates are fairly good at detecting when they are being strung along, and while most organizations cannot afford to be fully candid, candor should be your goal.

The worst-case scenario is that everyone within your organization works toward hiring what seems like the ideal candidate only to lose the candidate's interest through a lengthy offer process. While this may not be entirely your fault as you attempt to keep all decision-makers on task, if that happens, blame often falls on the hiring manager. It is also helpful to keep decision-makers and the offer process on task by keeping track of variables that could hamstring the offer process.

For example, is a key decision-maker going on vacation soon? I have seen unexpected vacations derail offer processes. Summertime, November, and December are the common months for family vacations. I have had to wait for an offer to get certain approvals because the key approver was on vacation. Situations like this are avoidable. There must a backup manager to sign off on the offer.

Maybe the division or company has no budget in place to make this hire. Again, I have seen companies find a candidate they love, be ready to make the offer, and then discover the budget is no longer there. Do not let that happen to you. Try to find out what other opportunities the candidate may be considering as well. There may be another schedule that is competing with yours. Communication and proactivity are the words you live by in the offer process.

The hiring manager or the talent acquisition partner should be the person to deliver the offer to the candidate. Hopefully, you have continued conversation with the candidate and have kept in regular contact. If the offer preparation lasts from a few days to a week, one email to check-in is sufficient. Hopefully you have continued the rapport, so the candidate is excited to hear from you with the offer. When delivering the offer, try not to make compensation and benefits the focus. There will likely be some negotiation about that, but there is no reason to make money the focus of the initial discussion. Instead, focus on the opportunity, the career path, and the team the candidate will be joining. Engage the candidate so that when the discussion about compensation begins, your potential hire is already envisioning themselves in the role.

If offer preparation exceeds one week, talk to HR and seek solutions for how to shorten the process so that great talent would not be lost.

However, do not adopt the mind-set that you have reached the end of the evaluation process once an offer is made. While this is a significant step, be aware of any potential red flags in the offer presentation. While it is unusual for red flags to emerge at this stage, you may see things that were well hidden during the evaluation process, such as statements about what the candidate values, or aspects of how they really communicate in a business setting. Your job as an evaluator does not end simply because an offer was made. After receiving the offer, a talent will evaluate the offer thoroughly, and oftentimes they negotiate. What and how they negotiate normally reveals a person's values and belief systems. Some people are greedy and keep asking for a better offer. Some people are focusing on short-term gain rather than long-term opportunity. They negotiate and if the result is not ideal, they walk away and may regret it later.

For this reason and others, you should keep backup candidates and contingency plans in place. Discuss these backup plans with decision-makers in the hiring process so that you can be flexible with your offer process. Understand the parameters of what is available for compensation negotiations and the scope of your authority in those negotiations. Keep in contact with all candidates who could ultimately end up being hired. The recruiting cycle is not truly over until a candidate has accepted an offer. Even then, I would not formally notify other candidates in consideration that you hired someone else until the candidate you hired walks through your doors on day one. The war for talent is fierce, and I have seen candidates approached by competitors before their first day of work. Even worse, after receiving the offer but before the start day with a new opportunity, some talents may change their minds and decide to go somewhere else. Disappointed and shocked, the hiring manager is left empty-handed, unless they have a great backup candidate to consider immediately. Indeed, it is not unusual for candidates to play offers against each other. Employers are doing all they can to attract top talent, and even though they may know the talent has received other strong offers and possibly has accepted another position, they may still try to get the talent sign with them. While I believe this is unethical, especially on the talent's part, and advise all my candidates against it, I have seen it.

If there are four to six weeks of onboarding processes, including background check, giving notice, relocation, and the like, it is imperative to stay in touch with the new talent on a weekly basis. Anything could happen before the talent starts the position. The art of being proactive is to be ahead of the game and mitigate any business risks through thoughtful planning and engagement.

Being proactive in this process also creates intangible values among all the talents who participated in the application, interview, and selection process. If people feel respected and impressed by how the company takes care of the job applicants, they will recommend other people become followers of the company.

Being proactive in this process also means engaging with all internal stake holders. For hiring managers, this could mean keeping other teams posted on this new team member or discussing any looming challenges about acquiring your next new talent based on what you have experienced during this time with your key team members or your HR business partners. For example, you may have realized that your current team members are more senior than the external applicants and yet their titles or compensation are not competitive at all. This is alarming because you are at risk of losing your team members, as they are fully aware of the same thing after interviewing with the new hire and other applicants. Issues like this need to be raised immediately, but it takes time to address them. The entire talent acquisition process is like a mirror that reflects not only your ability to acquire talents but also how competitive your company is in regard to retaining those top performers.

The bottom line is that as the final and most critical process in hiring, the offer process must be proactive and involve constant communication with both candidates and your internal decision-makers. In the end, you also must implement a review process to address and act on any business challenges that arise during the process, so do not overlook this key step.

CHAPTER 9

OBSTACLES IN ACHIEVING AN EFFECTIVE POWER RECRUITING PROCESS

B ased on my decades of experience, I've outlined the steps to an effective hiring process in the biopharmaceutical field to help you recruit top talent for your team. So, what are some common pitfalls I see in the process and how can you avoid them?

Not Having an End Goal in Mind

Recruiting requires a winning mind-set. It is essential to equip yourself with this mind-set before setting forth any strategies or processes of talent acquisition. It is never easy to acquire the talent you want. Your top talent will be other hiring manager's top talent too. If they are not, you probably should not hire them anyway. So, it is a very competitive game and involves many moving parts. A lot of these changing dynamics and challenges are not within your reach or control. But be confident and optimistic and infuse the same level of passion that you have put toward your work into hiring your talents. Be clear in your vision and goals in bringing this talent aboard. Visualize the day that your talent is with you on your team. How could he or she add to the bottom line of your team? What is the direction that you want this person to go toward with your business strategy set for the team? What is the culture that you want to create, reinforce, or change? Be optimistic. Be confident. If you answer these questions with great clarity and positive energy, you will have this person working for you soon.

Poor Job Descriptions

So now that you have a clear vision of your team, what is next? Everything still seems uncertain. You start to ask many questions, such as where can I find the person and how can I close this role? While all these are immediate questions to ask, the number-one question is how can I develop an effective job description that communicates well with potential talent out there? If anything else is uncertain, at least we know developing a good job description is within your reach.

While this was addressed in Chapter 5, I cannot stress the importance of the job description enough. The main purpose of a job description is to attract the right applicants and eliminate the wrong ones. Poor job descriptions are the biggest source of problems in the recruiting process. A poor job description can be too general or too narrow; it could be a leadership role that does not reflect responsibilities of leading a team. Take the time to talk it through with the incumbents or key stakeholders who interact extensively with this role. Equally important, make sure the recruiters understand your job description.

Also, if there are aspects in the job description where there is some give, make sure the recruiter knows that. If the job description is not right, it attracts wrong applicants or discourages the right talents from applying. Not only that, a poorly written job description can slow down the process. A recruiter needs to use the job description to communicate with the talent. If the job description is not accurate, the recruiting team can't start the recruiting process. A poor job description may also lead to wrong hires, affect employee morale, and increase the turnover. Poor communication with the recruiter about the job description is as great an obstacle as a poorly drafted job description.

Poor Communication between Recruiting and Hiring

Recruiting supports the business so that the businesspeople can focus on what they are best at, whether it is R&D or clinical or commercial development in the biotech industry. However, recruiting is a highly collaborate game that requires building strong partnerships between the business's hiring team and either internal or external recruiting support.

When there's an internal recruiting team, the hiring team should provide all the information relevant to the role to recruiting, such as an ideal profile, profiles to avoid, seniority, personality traits, daily responsibilities, business challenges in the coming months or year, career advancement opportunities, and so on. On the other hand, the recruiting team should advise on talent demographics, hiring trends, competition hiring info, compensation, possible challenges in recruiting and alternative solutions and creative ways to create interest. Hiring managers would love to learn about recruiting outside of their own expertise. The two parties should also discuss and confirm a recruiting process, including interview types, timelines, and expectations from one another during this first kick-off meeting.

Communication should stay open once the recruiting starts. During the process, it might be helpful to bring an HR business partner or another person from the business group to facilitate communication or address any issues along with the team.

Usually, if a position is very specialized or in a niche area, an external recruiting agency is engaged in helping with recruitment. Both the hiring manager and internal recruiter will partner with an outside recruiting specialist on a hire, whether it is an exclusive relationship or a general search sent out to multiple recruiting firms. It is important that you to stay in contact with those recruiters and communicate effectively with them. For example, deadlines must be communicated clearly. What is your timeline to fill this role? Working backward, let's figure out a timeline so we have a date for reviewing résumés and setting up the first phone interview and then on-site interview. The clearer you set up the timeline and communicate with your recruiters, the sooner the position gets filled.

When you set deadlines and meetings, you must adhere to them. Provide feedback on the candidates you receive. If the candidates are not good fits, explain why. Perhaps something is not being adequately communicated to your recruiting specialist or the vision you communicated to your recruiting partner needs refining. When you do find candidates who fit, communicate that to your recruiters and make sure to clearly communicate the timeline of the interview process. The recruiter will ultimately help to keep your candidate in the loop.

We once partnered with a hiring manager who was the vice president of commercial development at a billion-dollar company. His assistant helped him keep a spreadsheet of when he needed to see résumés, when he would conduct interviews, and so on. In order to meet the deadlines set, he also committed to get back to the recruiting team with feedback and push other team members for interviews. We had weekly calls to discuss recruiting progress and issues, and he addressed them almost right away. If not, he would get back in a timely way so we were all aligned on the strategy. If we had to adjust the recruiting strategy, we did so in a fast manner with his support. In the end, we filled all three senior-level marketing positions within his timeline.

Strong and ongoing communication helps everyone stay focused on the process to achieve the end goal in the most efficient manner. So, schedule a weekly call and reach out to your contact to share updates or thoughts. This actually leads to what we are going to discuss next—being transparent.

Challenges from Your Current Team

Oftentimes, there are other factors that may impede the recruiting process. For example, in the past I worked with a large pharmaceutical company that had a very high turnover rate among experienced directors. The problem was that there was a very flat structure at the top. The career ladders that were present at other competitors simply were not there for senior directors and executive directors. This made it extremely hard to replace those experienced directors with external talent. In situations like this, we like to consult with our clients to explain the potential difficulties in the hiring market. In the end, it was more sensible to promote internally. While it did not mean replacing senior-level employees with equally experienced talent, it did mean the company was able to promote talent that already had relationships with key stakeholders and knew the products well. In the end it was a win-win between the company and the internal employee.

We have also faced compression issues. For example, working in a fast-growing biotech company for many years, an internal employee would have experienced a very steep learning curve over the course of high-growth years. Meanwhile, the company kept a very flat team structure. When you hire an external talent, the hiring manager almost always has to pay more for someone whose skill sets are not as strong as the internal employee's. Or they end up not hiring because it would create an internal inequality.

In situations like this, you can probably anticipate when you have an ideal candidate in mind and invite your HR business partner for the discussion. How can this be addressed when the team needs to continuously hire talent externally to keep up growth? It seems like promoting current employees or adjusting their levels would be preferable to hiring externally.

Problems Sourcing Candidates

Sourcing candidates is difficult and time-consuming, which is why hiring managers often turn to outside recruiters. One approach to getting more candidates to view your postings is to work on branding. Branding experts can help raise a company's profile immensely. Another solution when you're experiencing a lack of candidates is to lean on your network. Reach out to colleagues and see if they know people who may be a good fit. If you have an internal recruiting team, try to minimize the time you take away from sourcing. I cannot count the number of hours I spent as an internal recruiter in meetings and discussions, as opposed to sourcing and interviewing talent.

I used to support a biostatistician team as their talent acquisition partner. The team always had five to ten PhD-level statistician positions open. To fill this role, a recruiter was expected to develop an entire industry database, which is roughly about three to five thousand professionals. I knew it was impossible to do that given the time and tools available to me. I had to engage with agencies that specialized in this field. It turned out to be a wise decision, as most of these talents only work with recruiters—they are not applying for jobs on their own.

As discussed in Chapter 6, passive candidates and hidden talents can be other challenges. They are not active or visible. It takes tremendous effort and a rigorous system to recruit them. Building such system and having an effective recruiting infrastructure takes time. Seek out the most experienced and motivated recruiter to help you solve the issue, so that you can focus on building your business.

Difficulties Interviewing and Selecting Candidates

Interviewing and selecting candidates essentially presents three challenges: timeline, criteria, and decision-making. Keeping a timeline is critical and it is important throughout the process. Having a timeline should help keep everyone focused on reaching the final result. The timeline should be a little bit more aggressive so you are ahead of the curve in competing with other employers and accommodate other changes along the way. For example, a recruiting goal to hire a sales director of oncology is set to meet the timeline of being ready for a national sales meeting in January. When we plan the process, we would be looking at extending an offer in the prior December. This means interviews would need to take place in October or November due to the congested holiday season.

Interview criteria are guided by the job description for the hard skill sets. For the soft skill sets, you have to communicate to the interviewing team about what work ethics and personalities are desired and what type of culture is valued on the team. Make it consistent and develop a standard for someone to live by, even beyond the interview.

Selecting the right candidate is about making a final decision. There is often great disagreement about candidates among the interview team. How do you solve those disputes? While there is no one-size-fits-all approach that will do the trick, listen to the feedback from the different interviewers and then consult your own internal mental model of the ideal candidate. You have to understand what these differences are and why they occur. Try to avoid interview bias while thinking over all the different feedback. When I worked as an internal recruiter, I always participated in a debriefing call. Someone from a peer level would say, "The interview went well, but I am just not sure how interested the candidate is. He seemed a bit disengaged when we spoke." Another more senior member on the team could give the opposite feedback. You may also gather feedback within the network of people who used to work with this individual. If you receive mixed interviews, what do you do?

In situations like this, if you are not 100 percent confident about the talent, do not rush to make a decision. Create at least one other opportunity to interact with the candidate or an opportunity for the candidate to show initiative in the areas that you heard different feedback. No one is going to be liked by everyone. This is a fact that I have learned in working in the people business. The most likable candidate can turn out to be not that likable after he or she comes on the team. Someone you thought was ordinary could prove to be a superstar. People are complex. There is no system that can tell you who to hire. You have to stay focused on your vision for the team and the ideal profile of this position, and trust your gut feeling from when you meet them in the interview. Look below the surface, ask deep questions, and be authentic as a hiring manager so that the person at least feels that he or she can be authentic with you. Build trust through the process and provide plenty of opportunities for them to demonstrate. At the end of the day, as a hiring manager, you make the decision.

Along the way, do not be afraid to follow up with some of the psychometric tools discussed in Chapter 7. I have used these psychometric tools often, and I find that not only do they often validate the impressions of interviewers but the candidates are also usually excited to see the results. Data is your friend—the more of it, the better.

Declined Offers

No one likes declined offers, but they are a fact of the hiring world. If you truly like a candidate, think about how you can improve the offer if they decline it. There are a few ways to improve the offer acceptance.

Focus on sharing your passion and vision when you interview. Most of the top talent you want to pursue have a very strong sense of purpose. What I found in the biotech industry is that many people, especially after they have gained some experience, are very interested in working with smaller biotech companies, where most of the growth occurs in the industry. Sharing this passion and vision creates that immediate bond that will make your candidate feel energized. If you are working in a fast-growing biotech company and setting a high bar for your newly created team, the right talent means not only the right skill sets but also the right mentality and willingness to grow fast with you.

Talk about opportunities within the team and company and how you think the talent can take advantage of them. This takes you one step further to think on behalf of your talent. Why do they want to work for you and what could you offer? Where would you like them to be five years from now, and what does it look like within and outside your team? In the end, it is your people, not sales, numbers, or products, that are your greatest professional asset. Hire the best talent with the mind-set that you want. In return, they will help you build the team and take the company to the next level.

Create a competitive offer through partnering with HR. Imagine the candidate has two offers—one is a counteroffer from your current company and the other is an external offer from your competitor. How could you compete with that competitor? Is your company leading in compensation? If not, do you offer great benefits? If your monetary offer is not at least 50 percent above the market and you want to hire the top talent, think about all the points discussed earlier and provide something unique to the candidate that no one else is offering. It could be your personal coaching time. Demonstrate yourself as a leader in the area and attract the talent to work for *you*. Communicate a three-year development plan with your top talent. Discuss any possible solutions with HR if situations like these do occur.

Have at least one backup candidate and engage with your recruiter to continue interviewing candidates until the position is filled. This is our practice every time we take a search. Our end goal is to have two perfect candidates filling the job. We want to guarantee that after spending weeks of efforts filling a role, we would never be in the situation where we have to go back and start from scratch again. Having a backup candidate is the only way to avoid the risk of the candidate declining the offer.

While declining the offer is negative news to the hiring manager and HR, it could be a sign that all parties can learn something to help do a better job in the future. Perhaps a candidate really was not a good fit. If the company's value proposition is not a strong fit to attract experienced talent, maybe it's time to develop talent from within. Maybe the interview process took too long or maybe something happened during the interview. Maybe the candidate experience was not that great. Anyway, it is helpful to get the information through a follow-up conversation with the candidate.

When you have a declined offer, the most important thing is to move on. While the talent market is competitive, the right candidate is always out there for you.

Other Factors Impacting Recruiting Outcomes

Adaptability of the Recruiting Mechanism

For most organizations, recruiting is an ongoing business event. It is important to evaluate your company's recruiting mechanism on a regular basis. If a system has not been evaluated and changed for a long time, it is probably outdated. The purpose of changing and adapting is to make the system fit your current business needs. This involves, but is not limited to, reevaluating your strategies in sourcing, recruiting, and work processes, from reviewing résumés and scheduling candidates to, more importantly, assessing the partnerships and owners of different processes within this system.

Candidate Experience

A candidate may not have had a good experience when coming to interview at your company. They not only experience a tremendously long time scheduling an interview, but after the interview, they are not given any feedback. The interviewers ask random questions, and they are unprepared with the candidate résumés. The candidate is asked three times to be on-site, and one time, it is a five-hour interview. Examples like these sound extreme, but they do exist. In the biopharma industry, it is pretty much a candidate's market. So handle your candidates with great care.

Utilization of Technology in the Era of Digital and Social Media Recruiting

This is for the company still relying on job applications to receive applicants. Maybe there is no digital marketing strategy supporting talent acquisition to increase the employer's branding and attract passive candidates. Digital branding competitiveness is the major differentiator that can set apart your company from other competitors. If your company has not started yet, start your own branding as a hiring manager. Be visible and create some content on social media or in your network to attract that talent.

Adoption of Remote Interviewing and Hiring

Companies need to adopt remote hiring models to make their hiring process nimbler and more competitive. The talent market is vast and remote recruiting is a powerful tool in helping you access all the talent out there in the most efficient manner. It is incumbent on every hiring manager that they develop a remote interviewing and hiring process, with protocols set out for interviewers to follow. Take some time now to develop a remote interview methodology; try out the various remote interviewing platforms and see which you like best and utilize these tools on your next search. You will see that you capture more passive candidates who may not be willing to travel, and that the process moves much more smoothly with less scheduling and administrative headaches. Remote hiring is going to be the norm going forward.

CHAPTER 10
REFLECTIONS ON POWER RECRUITING

Hopefully this book has been a helpful guide for you to gain insights on the power recruiting system and help you navigate the hiring process to give you the best hire. Recruiting is constantly evolving, and I would like to conclude with some fundamentals that can be your strategies and guidelines to excel in this field. These can also serve as pointers when you work with your recruiting partner for a better hiring result.

In the journey of writing this book, I have also become more confident than ever that recruiting is a learned craft that we should all be proud of mastering. On a personal level, it demands your heart and soul to put the people in the right place and continue to develop them. On a professional level, it requires strong partnerships and systems to make these acquisitions reality. I would love to embark on this journey with you to recruit the best talent. I would also like to leave you with these key takeaways.

- **Have a clear and long view of your business and visualize who your talent is.** We have talked so much about this visualization process, and I can't say enough how it helped me become a top-rated recruiter in my career. In the end, you are building an incredible team by bringing your top talent onboard. The talent acquisition journey starts with you. Once the top talent is defined, it will find ways to come to you.

- **View your relationship with your recruiting team as a true partnership with candor and transparency.** You cannot hire candidates yourself. Effective recruiting comes from a strong partnership. In this partnership, you are not a hiring manager but a true leader in whose footsteps other people want to follow and whose business they want to support. Be authentic to communicate your management styles and be open to talking about the business challenges that could be solved by hiring a particular person. Have your Talent Acquisition or HR business partner understand you and your business. The more trust you put in this partnership, the better results you will see. Your recruiting specialist is typically a very busy recruiter who will make sure to put your priorities as their top priorities.

- **Keep the process simple, with a focus on implementing recognizable key milestones.** The milestones could be as simple as a timeline of critical recruiting stages, such as phone interviews, on-site interviews, and hiring. Advise all parties on these milestones and hold them accountable to deliver. This is exactly what we talk about when we talk about being proactive. Nothing gets done if it's not planned ahead. If you want to have a medical director onboard in April, an example of milestones would be:

    First week of February: candidate review (rolling basis)

    Second through fourth weeks of February: phone interviews and on-site interviews

    First and second weeks of March: wrap up on-site interviews; extend offers.

- **Have a fluid interviewing process so that people are moving along quickly in the process.** A fluid interview process means one that is open to changes when the process itself is holding things back in a particular circumstance. For example, do you need to meet candidates and find the time to schedule a final interview with your manager, as the entire month you will be traveling overseas? Can you do a Skype interview? If an interviewer was missed in the earlier interview round, would you reschedule the interview or provide another opportunity that could assess the talent skills in a similar way? Define each person's role in moving the process but create a system to be able to meet unexpected logistic challenges. Have a "Plan B" at all times.

- **Apply the 80/20 rule in recruiting too**. Cut off unnecessary processes and focus on people who support you in recruiting. Once you have the partnership in recruiting, focus on how you can delegate 20 percent of your time on recruiting so that your business will generate 80 percent more results. This means that you have to hire quickly and effectively. Hire the best of what is out there. To achieve this, spend more time with your recruiters on a regular basis. Sit down with your HR business partner to address the HR issues relative to current or future hiring. For example, do we create more career ladders for the team so that internal people are promotable to the next level quickly and thus increase the retention? All these efforts will pay off many times over down the road.

- **Plan your recruiting at least a year ahead.** If you have a business plan worked out a year or three in advance, recruiting should be part of that plan. Plan your hiring in advance and make sure it is part of the business growth strategy. Discuss plans with your recruiting partners. Pipeline candidates in advance. Cutting-edge and robust biotech companies do more than just campus recruiting—they actually approach passive candidates and invite them for on-site meetings or exploratory interviews months and years in advance. Building relationships takes time, and getting to know talent also takes time. So, start early, plan ahead, and integrate building relationships in your business plan. Discuss details with your recruiters and HR. They are the ones who are capable of drafting a detailed plan and implementing it to meet future business needs.

- **Explore passive candidates and have them want to work for you enthusiastically.** Be seen in social media as a hiring manager, especially on LinkedIn, or create a hiring manager video to attach with the job posting. This can be posted on your company's Twitter account, website, or similar outlets. A message from the hiring manager or one of your team members will be so much more powerful coming from HR. You will expand your outreach and build personal branding on social media. The other way to explore passive candidates effectively is to share your hiring needs during conferences or meetings with industry experts. Broadcast your hiring needs. Schedule one-on-one meetings with people who you are familiar with. This will grow your network and find the talent you can trust in that network.

- **Review and evaluate your recruiting as a business function periodically.** As recruiting is constantly evolving along with the company, the external dynamics, and talent market, what works now may not continue to work in the future. For things that don't work, view them as an opportunity to get better. This is really about having the mentality of seeing recruiting and hiring as a value-creating process rather than a time-consuming and costly event. How often do you look at the business and evaluate it? Every six months? At least every year? View recruiting this way as well. Absorb the best practices and build your team's hiring system one step at a time. Let recruiting be the fuel to grow your team and talent.

- **Turn to experienced recruiters.** Start to expand your own network of recruiters, especially those in executive search agencies who share the same values toward talent and who have a strong track record in the industry as well as illuminating passion to serve your needs. Finding talent together is a delicate process and you need to trust the recruiters you work with. When I started out with Bongene, I did not have a list of clients to work with, yet thankfully a few of my valuable clients took a leap of faith in me. I gave all I had to help the business take off and then later built our proprietary process to attract top talent. My clients trust me because I am always reliable and truthful. Building that trust comes from dedication and the high standard of excellence we hold for performing this craft. If you have not found a recruiter you like, start looking, because building that mutual trust takes time.

In the end, recruiting is a process, not an ending. It is not only a result but also a mentality—a mentality of winning and achieving great things together. You should look for the best people to work for you or partner with all the time. This is recruiting! The future is unknown, but one thing is known—no matter what you do or where your company is headed, it will never stop looking for the best talent and will always need to develop its present talent. Keep this recruiter mentality and continue building good and effective relationships with your network, whether it is with your talent or recruiting partners. This is the essence of Power Recruiting.

ACKNOWLEDGMENTS

I started to write this book during Christmas 2019, when I had a break from running a very hectic business. Even though I wanted to share my experience about recruiting with professionals in the industry for quite a long time, writing the book itself has been an unbelievable journey that I have never experienced before. All I can say is that after this book, I would like to keep writing.

To my parents—without them, I would not have received what I consider the best education or have inherited their strong work ethic. Their integrity, kindness, and thoughtfulness have always been the principles to guide me go through the complexities of life. I am forever grateful that after I became a mom, they have continued to support me and my family in any possible way so that I had more time and energy to focus on my professional life and chase my dreams.

Special thanks to Angela Lauria, CEO and founder of The Author Incubator, for believing in me, as well as to David Hancock and the Morgan James Publishing team for helping me bring this book to print.

To my developmental editor, Andrae Smith, and my managing editor, Emily Tuttle—thanks for making the process seamless and easy.

To my family—without their faith and encouragement, this book would not come to fruition. I hope this book serves a purpose and lets my children know that anything is possible when you put your mind to it.

To me, I know this book is not an end, but a beginning, a beginning of learning more, growing more, and serving more.

THANK YOU

I am grateful that I get to work and partner with some of the most dedicated, motivated, and smart biopharma professionals who make the world a better place to live through their work.

I would like to thank all the people who are dedicated to serving in this industry by hosting a bi-weekly webinar of my Power Recruiting System and offering a free consultation each week on hiring effectively and other relative topics.

If you're interested, please schedule a one-on-one call on our website, www.bongenesearch.com or email us at bongene@bongenesearch.com for more details.

ABOUT THE AUTHOR

 Diana Ji is the founder and president of Bongene Search, a dedicated global executive search firm in the life science sector. Diana established the firm in 2014 to build on her passion to serve the talent acquisition needs of biopharma companies. At Bongene Search, Diana developed and implemented the STAR recruiting process and Power Recruiting System to rigorously guarantee a high-quality hire every search.

Diana started her recruiting career in China in 2002. With her sharp mind and strong entrepreneurial spirit, she ventured into the executive search field and quickly became a top selling retained search recruiter. She then moved on to work in corporate HR with several Fortune 500 companies, as well as with a fast-growing biotech company in New York.

Diana holds a Master's in HR Management from the Rutgers School of Management and Labor Relations, one of the top MHRM programs in the United States. She resides in Edison, New Jersey, with her husband, two kids, and her lovely mini goldendoodle, Luna. She is passionate about music education, and community service through music and art programs. She is a violinist in the Edison Philharmonic Orchestra.

CPSIA information can be obtained
at www.ICGtesting.com
Printed in the USA
JSHW021148100321
12420JS00001B/37